New directions in geography teaching

Papers from the 1970 Charney Manor conference

Edited by **Rex Walford**
Principal Lecturer in Geography,
Maria Grey College, Twickenham

Longman

Longman Group Limited
London

*Associated companies, branches and representatives
throughout the world*

© Longman Group Ltd 1973

First published 1973

Paper edition ISBN 0 582 31240 X
Cased edition ISBN 0 582 31241 8

Printed in Great Britain by
Hazell, Watson & Viney Ltd, Aylesbury, Bucks

New directions in geography teaching

Contents

New developments in geography and their impact on schools
A conference held at Charney Manor, Berkshire, 1970

Participants and their posts at the time of the conference

MRS E. AMBROSE	Varndean Grammar School for Girls, Brighton
P. J. AMBROSE	University of Sussex
J. R. BALE	Nobel School, Stevenage, Herts
R. A. BEDDIS	Avery Hill College of Education, London
T. BENNETTS	Queens School, Bushey, Herts
MISS V. BEYNON	Kidbrooke School, London
MISS M. CAISTOR	Hove County Grammar School, Sussex
C. J. COLTHURST	Lancing College, Sussex
J. A. EVERSON	H.M.I.
B. P. FITZGERALD	St Dunstan's College, Catford, London
D. GOWING	St Matthias, Fishponds, Bristol, College of Education
G. H. HONES	University of Bath
P. S. HORE	Walworth School, London
J. A. HUSAIN	Barking College of Technology
MISS S. JONES	Colston's Girls School, Bristol
MISS M. KNIGHT	Brighton and Hove High School (*student teacher*)
C. A. JOSEPH	Marlborough College, Wiltshire
MISS P. LOGAN	Henbury School, Bristol
R. NEWMAN	Wandsworth School, London
J. REYNOLDS	Schools Council Project Associate, University of Bristol
R. ROBINSON	City of Birmingham College of Education
MISS R. ROBSON	Eastbourne County School for Girls
J. ROLFE	Haberdashers' Aske's School, Elstree, Herts
D. SOWTER	Plaistow Grammar School, London
G. STEVENS	Forest Hill School, London
W. V. TIDSWELL	Hereford College of Education
R. A. WALFORD	Maria Grey College of Education, London

Introduction

'Most of the stuff that I have read about the "new geography" has been either well above school level or else so full of waffle that how people have applied it in school is beyond my comprehension.' So wrote one baffled teacher from overseas recently. His view, perhaps based on an extravagance or two in recent academic journals, is understandable.

But it would not be shared by the contributors to this book. Though they are separated in some cases by quite major disagreements, they are united in the belief, apparent in the pages that follow, that new geography is something more than a mirage in the current geographical desert. In taking new developments seriously, the writers of the papers and lesson units that follow have also attempted to relate these quite practically to the world of the classroom – to apply new geography in school situations.

It is less than ten years since the first of the Madingley seminars was arranged for teachers. These seminars seem to be the generally accepted starting-point in Britain for the dissemination of new geography into colleges and schools, and since then experiments and innovations have gone on apace in all kinds of educational institutions up and down the country. It has inevitably taken time for experiments to be set up and to be tested, to be tried and to fail, and then to be revised and tried again. It is hardly surprising that only now, after a generous time-lag, is material related to the practical development of new geography in schools becoming available.

This collection may still therefore claim to be among the relatively early published material in this sphere, although it represents only a tiny fraction of the work which is currently going on in classrooms in Britain. It stems from a conference held in 1970 at which innovating teachers met and exchanged lesson experiences and ideas. The conference opened with a valuable contribution from a university geographer on the panorama of new developments in the subject and concluded with a searching discussion about objectives and curriculum. The conference consisted mainly of severely practical illustrations of what new geography meant to particular teachers in their attempts to interpret some of the material being made available from the universities. And though many of the teachers still had reservations about their own materials, they agreed that the publication of their materials might be useful to others searching for new ideas and interested in current developments.

The term 'new geography' is one that both practitioners and opponents would be happy to lose. Many of the ideas are certainly not new and (the opponents would say) perhaps some of them are not geography – in the sense that geography had been traditionally interpreted. But terms are at their least useful when being endlessly defined or delineated, and there is little doubt that most people now know what approach is meant when the phrase is used.

New geography as a term is usually applied to that loose collection of ideas which revolve around models, hypotheses, quantitative techniques, concepts and percepts. In terms of Pattison's 'four ways of geography' it is more likely to see geography as strong in terms of its spatial analysis theme than any other. Norton Ginsburg expressed the general ground swell succinctly in his introductory address to the International Geographical Congress at New Delhi in 1968:

> There has indeed been a major revolution in geographic thought and research during, say, the last thirty-five years or so and particularly in the last twenty . . . Contemporary human geography has become increasingly behaviouristic. It has also tended to focus ever more on problems relating to one of the four major dimensions of human organization, the spatial. At the same time research has moved rapidly, albeit erratically towards the formulation of general propositions and theories of organization and behaviour and away from preoccupation with patterns, per se. In this sense geography's internal organization and intellectual apparatus have come to resemble those of the other social sciences whereas formerly they were markedly at variance with them.

Ginsburg, later in his address, went on to refer to the 'beginning of a new age for geography as a full-fledged member of the social science fraternity'. He suggested that the 'future of geography as a major research discipline will be determined on the intellectual battlefields of the universities, where competition and conflict are immense; and where ideas are the hallmarks of achievement.'

It is perhaps this concern about ideas in geography that mostly pulls new geographers together whether thay are radical or reluctant about quantification, whether they are imaginative or immobile about model-building. If geography is to survive in the school curriculum it will have to be more than a convenient examination-pass for those who seek only to memorize a jumble of facts and sketch-maps. The injection of exciting and challenging ideas through some of the newer techniques and topics appears to have possibilities not merely for the high-flyers in our sixth forms, but for the Newsom school-leavers as well.

This last point emphasizes another underlying strength of the new ideas. The thinking of educators like Bruner and Hirst gives a solid foundation to the intuitions of early practitioners. Bruner's concern with a structure of ideas and a 'spiral curriculum' is well in accord with a geography which grapples with some central ideas and which is strong in depth rather than breadth. Indeed, it is this perspective which allows some discrimination in the acceptance of ideas first propagated at the research level; not all Ph.D theses need instant transmission down the educational line.

It would be idle to pretend that the new geography yet adds up into a complete philosophy; the variance of views within this book proves that. Nevertheless it is already something more than just a bright new box of tricks. The discussion in Part 2 of this book is one which will have been carried further by the time this collection is in print.

In view of the current trends towards inter-disciplinary studies, this re-grouping of geographical forces may be timely. At any rate, some schools in parts of Britain (hailed on many sides as showpieces for all that is best in English education) have lately begun operations without a geographer on their staff. This decision is apparently based on the belief that geography, as at present taught in schools, is hardly an essential element of a forward-looking curriculum – whether it is taught as a separate subject or as part of an interdisciplinary curriculum. A rediscovery of the ideas at the heart of the subject may help to identify the particular contributions that the geographer can make, now that his former staple recipe of snippets of world information can be better provided by TV, an encyclopaedia or even a comic book.

Most contributors to this collection, however radical, would not suggest that this means abandoning all 'old geography'. What is in disrepute is what old geography, haunted by the spectre of fact-dominated examinations, has turned into. Ideas in geography need to be clothed with the colour of eloquent description, the genuine curiosity of place and the appreciation of landscape. But these things do not make a subject in themselves – and their 'external linkages' may place them more sensibly in the realms of other subjects unless they adhere to identifiable cores of ideas.

Ahead lies a long period of transition and adaptation, as new geography finds its level within the frameworks and the capabilities of those who teach geography; but those who write in this collection would all feel that a start has been haltingly but necessarily made.

De Bono's desire to put thinking as a subject on the curriculum might be partially answered by a swing towards 'a geography of ideas' as envisaged by some contributors in this book. This momentum was clearly expressed by Neville Scarfe almost twenty years ago in his observation that 'Geography should be a light in the mind and not a load on the memory.'

The book is divided into two distinct parts. In Part 1, set out with intro-ductions and teaching material, are a dozen 'units of work' which have been used in the classroom by teachers. All the units stem in some degree from the impetus of recent developments in geography. These twelve units represent some if not all of the themes discussed in papers in Part 2. A reader completely unacquainted with such themes might prefer to read the papers by Ambrose, FitzGerald, Walford and Everson before tackling the teaching units.

Detailed descriptions are included with each of the twelve units. It is worth noting, however, that all age-ranges from eleven to eighteen are covered within the examples, and that several of the units have been taught with mixed ability groups. The teachers involved are from comprehensive, grammar and independent schools and the work has done with all-boy, all-girl and mixed classes.

The emphasis on the testing and operating of models is apparent in a variety of contexts. Sheila Jones's exercise on the testing of a version of the Von Thunen land-use model for younger pupils contrasts with the sixth-form work of John Rolfe in testing the urban models of Burgess, Hoyt, and Harris and Ullman. In the latter exercise, the field work integral to the project underlines the continuing desire to link classrooms with outside environment.

Both the Von Thunen and urban models are static in conception. A good deal of other work reflects the concern of teachers to examine the dynamic models that relate to process. FitzGerald and Stevens' simple iron and steel game shows this concern in the context of changing locational factors. Joseph's settlement game, in a more compressed time context, seeks to relate settlement, administrative boundaries and communications. Both these exercises are examples of the technique of simulation in which, to give additional insight, pupils are asked to put themselves in the place of decision-makers. Margaret Caistor's role-play exercise concerning town-development and water-resources is another example of this in a free-form situation. Beyond original basic biographies given to the participants (in this case lower-sixth-form girls) the simulation runs without rules. The emphasis here is on understanding the interplay of factors and viewpoints which leads to geographically important decisions.

The emphasis on understanding the decision-process has led to other avenues of exploration. Rex Walford's exercise investigates the influence of people's perceptions on their decision-making by attempting to discover the basis of such perceptions. From such exercises, conducted at a simple local level, it can be seen that men's images of the environment are frequently different from a supposedly objective view; and consequently their relationship with the environment cannot be presented in cut-and-dried stimulus-response terms.

Quantitative work is represented by Roger Robinson's exercise on random sampling of land-use maps and the subsequent testing of the results to see if there is significance. It is also represented by a physical geography exercise developed by Chris Colthurst for a unit on glaciation. Both these exercises, in their different spheres, aim to demonstrate that in certain situations the precision of quantitative work can lead not only to more satisfying conclusions but to the development of other possibilities not easily seen.

The 'generation of hypotheses' which results from the revealing of possibilities is clearly an important tool in focusing attention on particular geographical problems. The testing of such hypotheses, as in FitzGerald's Stewart Farm exercise, can become a rigorous, challenging and intriguing piece of work. The techniques associated with hypothesis testing and scientific method are related to problem-solving, and the field-work approaches suggested by both FitzGerald and Tidswell in the last two sections of Part 1 reflect this for both rural and urban environments. Problem-solving is also the applied geographical approach that Tidswell uses in his linking of three problems of accessibility for an exercise for thirteen- to fourteen-year-olds. It accords closely with the plea, often heard, to make geography relevant as well as rigorous.

Part 2 of the book is a collection of papers and smaller fragments which relate the wider implications of new developments in geography to the classroom. These include contributions from a university teacher and college of education lecturers as well as from practising teachers. The papers range from the discussion of developments at the research frontier to the presentation of pieces of experimental school curriculum; from discussions of educational objectives to suggestions about how to introduce new ideas into large school geography departments.

The paper by P. J. Ambrose outlines most of the current trends in the new geography in the universities. The themes which he generally surveys are taken up more specifically by the next three contributors.

Brian FitzGerald considers the impact of scientific method and quantitative techniques on approaches to investigations. Rex Walford discusses some of the problems encountered in the translation of model and simulation ideas to the classroom. John Everson's paper is concerned with the development of hypothesis testing specifically in relation to field work.

Gerry Hones raises many of the problems which occur in examining and evaluating the kind of ideas which are discussed above. He points out the difficulties which our present examination system creates and makes clear the effort, energy and clear-headedness that are needed to develop better and more wide-ranging testing procedures.

Then follow some short pieces on various aspects of the practical problems associated with the developments of new ideas. Peter Hore reports on a year's research spent testing the efficacy of some new geographical ideas (one of the few pieces of work so far written in thesis form). John Bale contributes a 'fragment' of a curriculum – four pieces of work linked together as part of a new-style North America course. The next three contributors consider the problem of new ideas into school situations. Graham Stevens outlines a simple and practical approach to the introduction of a new idea into a school department; Margaret Caistor writes of the way in which new ideas were added to an existing syllabus; Sheila Jones describes the development of a whole new syllabus, made possible by the flexibility of an examining board.

The final chapters in the book open up some deeper matters, which lie behind the practical problems outlined earlier. Rex Beddis considers the problem of appropriate content for the school curriculum and both David Gowing and Trevor Bennetts examine critically existing objectives, where identifiable. John Everson goes on to suggest a way in which a new curriculum might be evolved, based on carefully prepared matrices of exercises and Rex

5

Beddis offers, as a gloss on this idea, a plea for the retention of an areal (regional?) framework as a bridge between old and new.

Readers of this volume may approach it from different standpoints. Reader A may have heard much about the new geography from a theoretical viewpoint and be anxious to see if it can be realistically translated into satisfying activity for twelve-year-olds. Reader B may be a veteran enthusiast in the practical aspects, but wish to read more of the possible implications for curriculum or for evaluation and assessment. Reader C may have become vaguely aware of something stirring in the geographical undergrowth and felt that it might be helpful to read something about it which related generally to secondary school teaching.

One hopes that in each of these cases the collection of materials from the Charney Manor 1970 conference will have something to offer. Teachers, always aware that their materials are in a state of change and imperfection, have been generous in agreeing that extracts from their lesson materials should be published. In this way the classroom impact of new developments can begin to be assessed. No one would deny that here are only preliminary explorations; nevertheless, the papers in Part 2 point to the immense potential that has been revealed in the last ten years, as fresh ideas have given fresh vigour to geography as a school subject.

Part One

Teaching Units

I The iron and steel game†

The iron and steel game was originally developed by B. P. FitzGerald at St Dunstan's College, Catford for use with first-year (eleven- to twelve-year-old) pupils of a wide range of ability. The version reproduced here is an adaptation of the original idea by Graham Stevens, of Forest Hill School, S.E.19.

At Forest Hill, the game is used in the second year (twelve- to thirteen-year-olds) with all ranges of ability in a comprehensive school. In a 'concentric-style' syllabus, it follows field study of Thames-side heavy industry and the study of coal mining in South Wales. It is followed by a case study of the Spencer works, Newport, and by study of the locations of steel works in the UK and in the north-eastern USA. The game aims to develop concepts about industrial location which can later be related to actual locations, and to lead to a better understanding of some of the factors in the process of decision-making.

At Forest Hill, the game is used in the following way:
Lesson 1: The technical background sheet is given out. With less able pupils, it is read out and difficult words explained. Then the multiple-choice test sheet is given out, and, allowing the use of the technical background sheet, pupils are asked to complete the test sheet in ten to fifteen minutes. Pupils then correct their own copies, and those with the highest marks are elected chairmen of four to five companies. They then select or are assigned fellow board members from the pupils in the class. The amount of explanation about companies, shareholders, board meetings, directors, etc., varies with the ability and background of the class. (With less able pupils, reference to current TV series, e.g. *The Troubleshooters*, proves useful for role identification.)
Lesson 2: The furniture in the classroom is re-arranged so that company boards sit together. Map 1 is given to each board, along with sheet 1. The boards discuss amongst themselves and the teacher aims to be recessive, acting merely as adviser (if needed) and timekeeper. After time allowed for discussion, voting and recording, companies announce their decisions, and a profit or loss sheet is consulted. (Some teachers prefer not to assign particular financial consequences to the decisions taken, and merely to discuss what seem suitable and unsuitable locations on the evidence available.) Company results are written on the blackboard for comparison. Round two and round three follow in similar fashion. At the end of the game, winning should be under-stressed and the ideas that the game produces should be discussed.
Lesson 3: The three hypotheses about location developed by the game can be used in conjunction with a map of coalfields, iron-ore fields, and works locations to develop classifications of the UK and the north-eastern USA. A case-study of the Spencer Works at Newport emphasizes some of the greater complexities of the real-world situation.

†B. P. FitzGerald and G. Stevens

Response and evaluation
Forest Hill report that 'both staff and pupils are very enthusiastic about the game. The retention of important concepts appears to have greatly improved as a result. All pupils have gained from the discussions, and the need to make co-operative decisions.'

With some less able classes, it may be wiser to use the whole class as one company, so that the decision-making process is entirely corporate.

Technical background of the iron and steel industry (Sheet A)
Before 1750 Pig iron was smelted using iron ore, limestone and charcoal (baked wood). From 1700 to 1750 the coke (baked coal) furnace was developed by the Darby family in Coalbrookdale, Shropshire. The early furnaces were not very efficient and it took about 8 tons of coal to smelt 1 ton of iron.
1800–1856 Improvements to the furnace reduced the quantity required to smelt 1 ton of iron to 4 tons of coal by 1850. The improvements were closing the top of the furnace to use the gases produced and heating the air before it is blasted into the furnace.
Steel was hardly produced before 1856 since it was expensive, and cast and wrought iron were the main products. Steel is different from iron in being lighter, stronger and chemically it contains less carbon.
1856 Henry Bessemer invented his converter to make pig iron into steel cheaply. Air containing oxygen (O_2) is blown through the molten pig iron where it combines with the carbon (C) forming carbon dioxide (CO_2) which is given off.

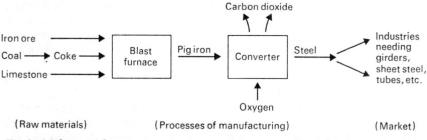

Fig 1. Making steel

Non-phosphoric ore All these processes could only use ore that does not contain phosphorus, which makes steel brittle. The main sources of iron ore at this time were 'black-band ore', which can be brought up from the same mine-shafts as coal since it occurs in the coal measures – the shales and sandstones in which the coal seams lie.
1867 Siemens-Martin open-hearth furnace was developed which could make steel more accurately and could also use 'scrap' steel.
1878 Gilchrist and Thomas basic process which lines the furnaces with material that absorbs phosphorus so that now many new low-grade phosphoric ore-fields in Britain could be used.

Twentieth century By 1960 half of the iron-ore used in Britain was high-grade from Canada, Sweden, Venezuela and North Africa. The use of oil and oxygen further reduced the need for coal to 1 ton of coal for 1 ton of steel.

Many steel furnaces use 70 per cent scrap like those in Sheffield and the West Midlands. In 1967 the industry was re-nationalized.

Do-it-yourself exercise to discover prospective chairmen of the five iron and steel company boards (Sheet B).

Using the written material on Sheet A answer the questions below by underlining the correct one. Your teacher will tell you the correct answers afterwards. The pupils with the highest marks will be obvious choices for responsible jobs on the Company Boards.

1 Pig iron is made in (a) open-hearth furnace (b) Bessemer converter (c) blast furnace
2 To smelt iron you need in addition to coke and iron ore (a) salt (b) limestone (c) wood (d) steel
3 The coke furnace for smelting iron was mainly used after (a) 1750 (b) 1867 (c) 1878 (d) 1902
4 It was invented by (a) Bessemer (b) Darby (c) Gilchrist (d) Thomas
5 In 1800 it took (a) 1 ton (b) 4 tons (c) 8 tons (d) 7 tons of coal to smelt 1 ton of iron
6 In 1960 it took (a) 1 ton (b) 4 tons (c) 8 tons (d) 7 tons of coal to smelt 1 ton of steel
7 The most important difference between steel and iron is that steel has less (a) oxygen (b) coke (c) carbon (d) iron ore in it
8 The main way this chemical is removed is by adding (a) oxygen (b) coke (c) carbon (d) iron ore
9 The invention in 1856 was (a) blast furnace (b) Bessemer converter (c) open-hearth furnace (d) basic process
10 The invention in 1878 was (a) blast furnace (b) Bessemer converter (c) open-hearth furnace (d) basic process
11 Most of the iron ore in Britain is low-grade and (a) non-phosphoric (b) phosphoric (c) fluorescent (d) haematite
12 In 1960 the amount of iron ore imported into the UK was (a) none (b) about half (c) three-quarters (d) all the ore required
13 It came from four of these countries (a) France (b) Canada (c) Spain (d) Belgium (e) Venezuela (f) Sweden (g) North Africa
14 Old established centres of the iron and steel industry like Sheffield and the West Midlands have run out of supplies of coal and iron but continue to make steel because of the skilled labour force and the fact that their steel furnaces can use over 70 per cent of (a) 'black-band ore' (b) Coal measures (c) scrap steel
15 The British iron and steel industry was re-nationalized in (a) 1956 (b) 1967 (c) 1867 (d) 1878

Iron and steel location
(Sheet 1)

The...Co Ltd

You have been divided into 4 or 5 groups of about 6 pupils. Each group of 6 makes up the Board of Directors of The...................................Co Ltd. The date is 1820. Your firm has £3,000 to spend on building an iron works in South Dunstanshire.

Write the name of the chairman and the rest of the board on the minutes sheet. Fig 2 has been prepared by the firm's surveyors to help you select the best site for the works.

The surveyor's report states that the three sites (A, B and C) have been selected because;

there is flat land to build upon

there is fresh water for use in processing

there are large villages nearby with many people with little work to do.

Now write down in (a) below what you and your neighbour think is the best site. Spend a minute or two discussing this with him. You will have to put forward your views at the board meeting afterwards. Remember the date is 1820.

Directors' board meeting Put forward your views, and try to convince the other members that your ideas are correct. Then a vote will be taken.

Votes for: Site A............... Site B............... Site C...............

Write out the minutes of the meeting below giving the reasons for the Board's final choice.

(a) Personal notes made between Mr..................... and Mr.....................

....

at a meeting at their club on 5 November 1820...

....

....

....

....

....

....

The...Co Ltd

(b) *Minutes of meeting held on 7 November 1820*

Those present: Chairman ....

Other members: ....

....

....

....

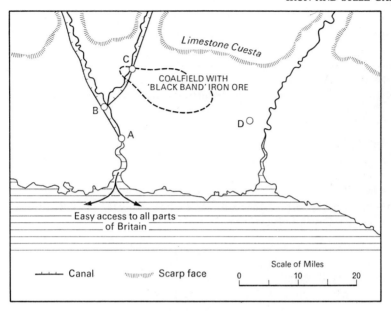

Fig 2. Surveyor's department 1820; map of possible locations

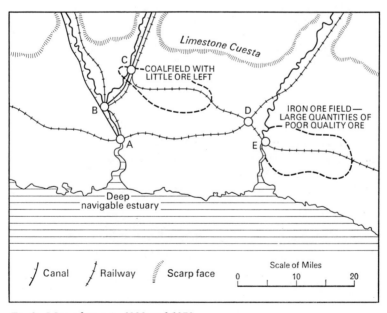

Fig 3. Map of area in 1880 and 1970

....

....

....

....

Voting: Site A................. Site B................. Site C..................

              Signed..

(Sheet 2)

The.............................Co Ltd has now – in 1880 – £15,000 to build a second iron works.

The last fifty years have been a period of great change – look at fig. 3.

The surveyor's report for 1880 with the map showing the possible sites A to E makes the following observations:

    (a) Quite large towns have grown up at A, B and C.

    (b) A new steel-making process for making steel cheaply, invented by Henry Bessemer, is now available.

    (c) A new iron-ore field, containing very large deposits, has been discovered about twenty miles to the south-east of the coalfield. Its iron ore is phosphoric, but though it occurs in great quantities it is of very poor quality.

    (d) The Gilchrist and Thomas basic process allows the furnaces to use this low-grade phosphoric ore.

    (e) Railways now connect towns A, B and C and main lines run to many other parts of Britain (see fig. 3).

Discuss the new situation as laid out in the surveyor's report with your neighbour. Then decide which location you think would be the best for the new plant. Below, at (a) give the reasons for your choice. Then be prepared to put forward and argue your point at the forthcoming board meeting.

Directors' board meeting During this meeting try to convince the other members of the board that your decision is the right one. After everyone has had the chance to speak a vote will be taken.

Site A.................. Site B.................. Site C..................

Site D.................. Site E..................

Now below the minutes write notes concerning the reasons for the board's decision.

(a) Some notes made during a conversation between Mr..........................
and Mr........................... on 3 December 1880.............................

....

....

....

....

14

The...Co Ltd
(b) *Minutes of the meeting held on 5 December 1880*
Those present: Chairman...
              Other members: ....
                            ....
                            ....
....
....
....
....
....

Voting: Site A.................. Site B.................. Site C..................
        Site D.................. Site E..................
                        Signed...

(Sheet 3)
The date is now 1970 and the board of directors of the ....
.........................Steel Corporation.. (some of whose great-great-grandfathers sat on earlier board meetings of the old manufacturing companies) has now an investment scheme for a large modern 'integrated' steel works, which will cost £20 million.
Again the problem is where to put it.
A number of points are important:
(a) Very cheap iron ore can be obtained from Canada and North Africa, but iron ore and coal can be obtained from the fields in South Dunstanshire.
(b) A great deal of water will be required for the new works – for use in making steel.
Should the corporation spend the money on adding to the works built in 1870 in an area of high unemployment? Or should it choose a new location? Discuss this decision with one of your board members and decide where you think the new works should be placed. Make a note below at (a) of the reasons for your decisions.
Directors' board meeting You should now argue the case for your decision, but you may change your mind if you think the reasons for selecting a site other than yours are good. The voting went as follows:
Site A.................. Site B.................. Site C..................
Site D.................. Site E..................
Now write the minutes below, mention what was said at the meeting and the reasons for the board's decision.
Do you think every board of directors would have come to the same decisions?
Yes............ Why?..
No .... Why not?..
Now look at fig. 58 in your text-book (Honeybone and Goss, *Britain and Overseas*), and complete the following table:

1 No. of coalfields	*2* No. of iron ore fields	*3* No. of iron and steel areas	*4* No. of steel areas on coalfields	*5* No. of steel areas on iron ore fields

Column 4 added to column 5 does not add up to the total number of iron and steel manufacturing areas in column 3. How many are left over? ....
Almost all of those not on coalfields or on ore fields have one thing in common. What are they all very near to?..
Where do you think they might get their ore from?.................................
Which of the three groups of iron and steel areas we have talked about do you think is the oldest and which the most recent?....................................
....

(a) Some notes concerning the forthcoming board meeting of the...............
....Steel Corporation.
Date 1970.
Conversation with Mr............................. ....
....
....
....
....
....

(b) Minutes of meeting of board of directors of.....................................
Steel Corporation, held at..on ....
Those present: Chairman..
　　　　　　　Others present: ....
　　　　　　　　　　　　　...
　　　　　　　　　　　　　...
　　　　　　　　　　　　　...
....
....
....
....

Results of Vote: Site A
　　　　　　　Site B
　　　　　　　Site C
　　　　　　　Site D
　　　　　　　Site E

　　　　　　　　　　Signed...

For teacher only (Use is optional)

PROFIT AND LOSS ACCOUNT: round one – 1820 as per computed results in business game

Location choice
(a) *Loss £1,000* 20 miles to carry 1 ton of iron ore and 8 tons of coal to furnace by canal to produce each ton of pig iron. Limestone has to be carried 30 miles. Poor location.
(b) *Loss £1,000* 10 miles to carry 1 ton of iron ore and 8 tons of coal to furnace by canal and horse and cart to produce each ton of pig iron. Poor location.
(c) *Profit £3,000* Both coal and iron ore are nearby and the canal can be used for collecting limestone and sending out the product. Best location.
(d) *Loss £3,000* 30 miles to carry 1 ton of iron ore and 8 tons of coal by horse and cart. Worst location.

PROFIT AND LOSS ACCOUNT: round two – 1880

Location choice
(a) *Loss £10,000* Coal from 20 miles to north and iron from 30 miles to east. Poor location.
(b) *Loss £10,000* Coal from 10 miles to north and iron ore from 40 miles to east. Poor location.
(c) *Profit £5,000* Coal nearby and even if 40 miles to iron ore this location has skilled workers, existing works, and possibly can use scrap steel. Second best location.
(d) *Loss £15,000* Coal from 30 miles north-west and iron ore from 10 miles south-east. Worst location.
(e) *Profit £15,000* Low-grade iron ore cannot be transported far and furnaces by 1880 now use less coal. This is the best location.

PROFIT AND LOSS ACCOUNT: round three – 1970

Location choice
(a) *Profit £21,500,000* Best location on a large flat site by tide-water, so high-grade iron ore can be imported cheaply. Less than 1 ton of coal per ton of steel is used now, so this is relatively less important.
(b) *Loss £21,000,000* Long way from tidewater, coal, iron and skilled labour. Poor location.
(c) *Profit only £500,000* Expensive to import iron ore from coast, and coal is now less important but skilled workers are here as well as existing works and scrap. The government might want to locate plant here to keep people

employed in the area and might give a £10,000,000 subsidy to the firm. A poor location though.

(d) *Loss £21,000,000* Long way from coal, iron ore, skilled labour and scrap. Poor location.

(e) *Profit only £1,000,000* Has skilled labour and scrap, but is distant from ore and coal. Poor location.

II Settlement game†

The settlement game unit as reproduced here is the version of C. A. Joseph of Marlborough College, Wiltshire, based on an idea of R. T. Dalton. It is used in a first-year (eleven- to twelve-year-old) course on the local region, but has also been used effectively with older pupils.

The game is designed to show pupils that the location of settlements depends on many interacting factors, some of which reflect the technology of earlier peoples. It also attempts to emphasize some of the complexity underlying settlement location that is not readily apparent from 'pure' study of the 1″ Ordnance Survey. Each pupil is given the information sheet and the map. Their aim is to build up a settlement pattern, a route network and a regional organization (parishes). The actual game takes only a single or double period, depending on ability. Follow-up is given as much time as the game itself, and involves comparison and discussion of the patterns evolved.

As used at Marlborough, the unit is followed by a tracing of parish boundaries from the 1″ to 1 mile OS map of the south side of the Vale of Pewsey (Sheet 167), and the plotting of settlements within the parishes. Shapes derived from the game are then compared with those derived from the map and reasons for the differences discussed. This (one hopes) leads on to an understanding of the local region in Saxon times, and so back to the actual settlements, and the factors affecting their locations.

Extension of the game

It is possible, of course, to make this a more sophisticated game with higher ability levels and age-ranges. Actual geological variation can be introduced as a factor, and mathematical weightings provided for the various factors.

An example of this can be found in chapter 2 of *Settlement Patterns* by J. Everson and B. P. FitzGerald (Longman).

Information Sheet

In the sixth and seventh centuries A.D. Anglo-Saxon settlers made their way to southern and eastern England. They came in small bands, usually peacably, to a country where little land had yet been cleared for cultivation. Their tribal organization was strong, so that their settlements were established as

†C. A. Joseph

clusters of houses around which lay arable land. But equipment was primitive, and although they had better ploughs than their predecessors, they could not cope well with areas of heavy soils. You must try and imagine an England immensely different from the present day. All land near rivers was liable to flood in winter, and most of the lowland was still forested. Only the lighter, sandy soils and such hills as the chalk downlands, would have been more open country with grass and shrubs.

The settlers had several needs, and must have chosen their sites carefully, for most of them have survived over 1,400 years to the present day. In order of importance their needs were:

1 Access to a constant supply of water. Water could not be carried.
2 Access to cultivable land. Travel wasted work time.
3 Avoiding waterlogged land. This was no use for crops or houses.
4 Access to woods. Timber was used for buildings and fuel, and acorns etc. provided food for pigs.

In order to meet these needs the settlements were spread about 1 mile apart in the best conditions, and 2 miles or more if the circumstances were worse.

The map (fig. 4) shows the sort of country that the Anglo-Saxons might have found. On this map:

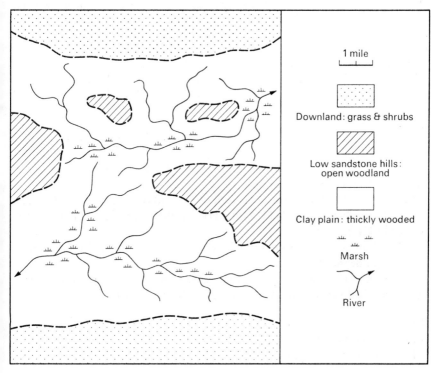

Fig 4. Map for settlement game

1 Mark suitable sites for 20 groups of settlers. But do not do this without considering questions 2 and 3 as well.
2 Mark possible routes for paths to connect the villages. Each village need be linked to only one or two others.
3 Each village had a piece of land shaped so as to give it a fair share of all the types of country nearby. Draw lines to show how boundaries might be created for all your villages.

III Stewart Farm†

This unit was devised by Brian FitzGerald at St Dunstan's College, Catford and used with a variety of first year (eleven- to twelve-year-old) classes in a British Isles course.

It is designed to follow up the previous consideration of the factors influencing the use of land (i.e. to tackle hypothesis-testing in a practical way – see Part 2, Ch. 2). The material reproduced below was given to the pupils in duplicated sheets, and after preliminary introduction of the material by the teacher, the pupils worked through the exercise at their own speed, with the teacher giving individual assistance as was needed. Following the work done in exercise books (see question 6) there was discussion of the answers given. The data was adapted from that gathered by personal field work. The unit took four, forty-minute lessons.

The unit is discussed further in FitzGerald's chapter on 'Scientific method, quantitative techniques and the teaching of geography' in Part II.

Stewart Farm

One of the suggestions you have made explaining why a farmer makes use of his land in different ways is that the slope of the land will affect the choices he makes. You have suggested that the steeper the slope the less value will be the crop or other land use to him.

Fig. 6 shows Stewart Farm at the foot of the Chiltern Hills. Marked on this map is the land use in each field. Also marked is the value of the land use to the farmer in £'s per acre.

Fig. 7 shows the same farm but with contours marked in and the steepness of slope (in degrees) for each field.

We will compare these maps to see if your suggestion is correct. However, before this is done the following tasks must be performed:

Tasks

1 Shade each field in fig. 6 in the colour suggested in the key. Shade very lightly – this is most important.

†B. P. FitzGerald

20

2 Shade lightly each field in fig. 7 in the colour suggested for the slope of land. This colour is suggested in the key.

3 Now turn to the table. For each field mark the type of land use in column 2, its degree of slope (see fig. 7) in column 3, and its value (see fig. 6) in column 4.

4 On graph paper construct the x and y axes of a graph thus:

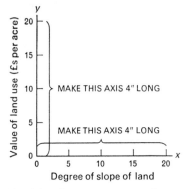

Fig 5. Graph of value of land (on the y axis) against degree of slope of land (on the x axis)

5 When you have constructed your axes, return to your completed table and now plot on the graph for each field its value of land use as 'y' and the degree of slope as 'x'.

6 Now answer the following questions in your exercise book.

(a) What would you say about the pattern made by the points on your graph? (If you can, draw a straight line through all the points but do not try to connect each point. We could call this a 'best-fit' line).

(b) What conclusion can you draw concerning the relationship between land value and slope?

(c) Three points on your graph do not occur near your 'best fit' line. This suggests that these three fields do not obey your conclusions. Use your maps to suggest why they do not.

1 Field No.	2 Land use	3 Degree of slope (x)	4 Value (y)	1 Field No.	2 Land use	3 Degree of slope (x)	4 Value (y)
1				9			
2				10			
3				11			
4				12			
5				13			
6				14			
7				15			
8							

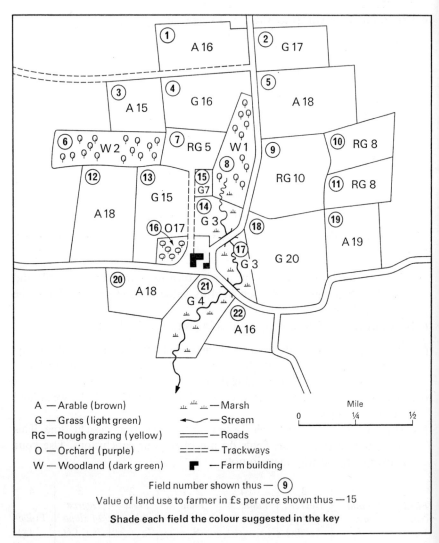

Fig 6. Stewart Farm, at the foot of the Chiltern Hills: land use and value

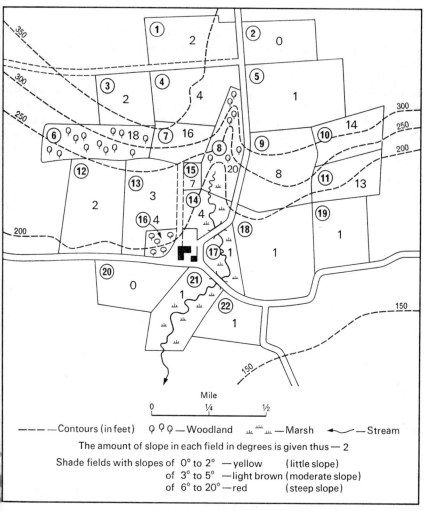

Fig 7. *Stewart Farm: slope of land*

IV Farming in the Sydney region†

This unit was devised by Sheila Jones at Colston's Girls' School, Bristol, and used in a second-year (twelve- to thirteen-year-old) course on agriculture. It is designed to illustrate the concept that land use around a large city can be seen to have a rough concentric pattern in some instances (i.e. a modern version of the local von Thunen model of land use). The material reproduced below was given to the pupils on duplicated sheets following an introduction from the teacher. The pupils worked at the problem at their own speed. The first lesson and homework were devoted to the completion and consideration of the exercise without any lengthy introduction. (As it was developed for second year pupils, instructions for shading were given in detail; for older pupils the exercise could obviously be modified to produce a greater degree of difficulty.) Homework marking was followed by discussion and by reference to other examples of the idea, using, for reference, *A sample geography of the British Isles* by A. Burrell and J. Hancock (Nelson) and M. Chisholm's *Rural settlement and land use* (Hutchinson).

The data and maps for the exercise were adapted from material in *New viewpoints in economic geography* by J. Rutherford, M. I. Logan and G. J. Missen (Harrap).

Farming in the Sydney region

1 Complete the three maps I, II and III, with the aid of the data sheet (see fig. 9).
2 Considering maps II and III, does there appear to be any pattern of land use around Sydney? If so, describe it.
3 Are there any notable exceptions in the pattern you have described? If so, describe where they are and, referring to the map of the physical areas, attempt an explanation.
4 Study Map II. Does this produce a pattern? Explain how the pattern is related to the distribution of types of farming established in maps II and III.
5 Suggest (giving reasons) how
   (a) the land between the city of Sydney and the L.G.A.s shown is used.
   (b) the land to the west of the L.G.A.s is used.
6 Using the city of Sydney as the centre of your diagram and the same scale as the map, draw a simple diagram to show the land use of the Sydney region.

†Sheila Jones

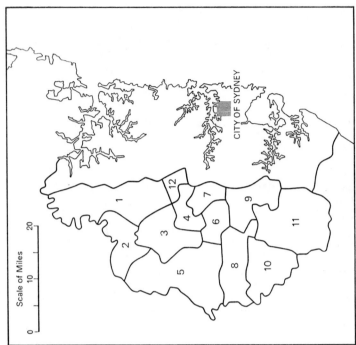

Fig 9. Sydney region: local government areas
(Three copies of this map were given to pupils.)

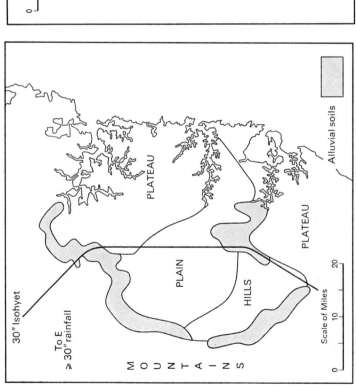

Fig 8. Sydney region: physical features

Farming in the Sydney region – Data sheet

Local Govt. areas	Average size rural holdings, Acres	% Cropland in vegetables + nurseries	Cows in milk
1 Baulkham Hills	39	22	2131
2 Windsor	67	40	1999
3 Blacktown	37	28	2737
4 Blacktown	17	73	1163
5 Penrith	172	20	7005
6 Fairfield	15	76	1013
7 Holroyd	7	91	127
8 Liverpool	78	17	1416
9 Liverpool	53	22	692
10 Camden	119	7	2597
11 Campbelltown	91	9	2962
12 Baulkham Hills	34	28	1193

All the areas shown have over 10% of their land devoted to agriculture.
For map I   Average size of rural holdings
Use 5 shadings of one/two colours and the following key:
0–35; 36–70; 71–105; 106–140; Over 140.
For map II   % Cropland in vegetables and nurseries
Use 5 shadings of one/two colours and the following key:
0–20; 21–40; 41–60; 61–80; 81–100.
For map III   Distribution of cows in milk
Use a symbol such as a dot or cross to represent 100 cows.

V   Accessibility in the Lake District†

This unit was devised by W. V. Tidswell of Hereford College of Education in connection with a course for the training of junior/secondary teachers in geography, and
was subsequently used in secondary schools with children of third-year (thirteen- to
fourteen-year-old) classes. It is designed to use a 'problem analysis' approach to try
to overcome the difficulties experienced by teachers of children of average and below
average ability. The 'problem' approach, as demonstrated in this exercise attempts
to:
(a) involve pupils in the assembling, processing and evaluation of data
(b) use data relevant to a recognizably real problem
(c) reveal that there is no exactly 'right' answer to many problems.
The instructions printed below are those for the guidance of the teacher rather than
for pupils. It is suggested that teachers work through the procedures step by step,
within a discussion framework. Tasks suitable for the pupils to tackle are specified.
    The data for the industries and employees comes from *Kompass*, a commercial

†W. V. Tidswell

directory published by Kompass Publishers, Croydon, Surrey and found in regional editions in public libraries. Past and present AA or RAC books may be useful as substitutes for basic census information, if the latter cannot easily be discovered. Any other map, brochure or guidebook material on the selected area would be useful. Local bus and rail timetables are essential pieces of supplementary data and can usually be obtained cheaply and easily by post.

Three problems in applied geography linked by a common theme: accessibility
Problem one
Mr Brown, an engineer, wishes to move from Birmingham to the Lake District, so that he can live in the country. Although he is a skilled engineer he is willing to work on the assembly line of any factory. Mr Brown has two teenage daughters who will have to rely on public transport to the nearest urban settlement for purposes of education and entertainment.
Suggested procedure for tackling the problem (teacher and pupils working together):
1 Consider the problem, analyse it, and break it into its component parts. What are the relevant factors? What data is needed?
2 Pupils construct a locational map of the main towns of the Lake District.
3 Pupils discover the past and present populations of towns from any sources which can be made available (Censuses? AA books? Atlases? Encyclopaedias?). Which towns are apparently declining, and which growing? What implications may this have for housing, future employment for Mr Brown, social and cultural amenities for his daughters?
4 Using *Kompass*, as a source, pupils list the industries to be found in each town (see example on page 29).
5 On the basis of 3 and 4 pupils select possible towns for Mr Brown to work in, and plot all the villages within a 10 mile radius of each. Is this the most appropriate radius? Discussion point.
6 How then to choose between villages? Introduction of the idea of an amenity index and an accessibility index. The amenity index may be determined by awarding points to each village for proximity to such attractions as historic places, places of scenic beauty, recreation centres. The accessibility index may be determined by using local bus timetables, and dividing the time taken (in minutes) to travel from the village to its nearest town by the daily frequency of the service. Pupils work out amenity and accessibility indices for the villages.
7 Pupils select possible villages in which Mr Brown and his family could live and put them in an order of priority.

NB A good deal of the geography of the Lake District will have been covered incidentally in this exercise.

Problem two
A bus operator in the Lake District wishes to plan a tour of the area so that

the maximum number of attractions may be seen when travelling a minimum distance. What route should he plan?

Suggested procedure for tackling the problem:

1 Pupils study maps, books, brochures, etc. and list the main tourist attractions of the Lake District.
2 Class discussion about the reasons that places are 'tourist attractions'. Consideration of lists and of differences within them. Can a rank order be established for the attractions? If so, on what basis?
3 Pupils plot agreed 'attractions' on a map.
4 Pupils consult maps of the road network of the area and determine the most economical route (i.e. the one which gives maximum value for minimum expense).

NB Route minimization is a complex process when dealing with a highly developed network, but in this area of adverse relief, there is, in fact, little choice of route possible.

Problem three

A multiple bakery manufacturer wishes to build a factory in the Lake District. From this factory, fresh bread will be delivered daily to all the towns. What is the best location for such a factory, presuming that the baker wishes to minimize his costs of distribution?

Suggested procedure for tackling the problem:

1 Preliminary study of a map of the area. Possible choice of a location by eye.
2 Pupils construct a 'mileage matrix' (see below). In the appropriate box they fill in the shortest road distance between each town and its neighbours.
3 From this, discuss which town appears most favourably placed to supply all the others in the area. Does this agree with the decision reached by eye alone?
4 Further discussion – relate back to what was found out about industry in Problem 1. Relate also to population factors. Might there not be a need for 'weighting' some of the mileages, in proportion to the size of the population of the towns? Would this make any difference to the decision reached in 3?

	Penrith	Keswick	Kendal	Ambleside	Windermere
Penrith	—				
Keswick		—			
Kendal			—		
Ambleside				—	
Windermere					—

Example of a mileage matrix (for part of the Lake District)

NB This problem introduces the theme of market size and distance from markets as factors in the location of industry. It may be useful at the end of this unit to go back to consider the pattern, scale and type of industry that the Kompass data reveals in Problem 1 (and see below).

Name of town	Name of factory	No. of employees	Name of town	Name of factory	No. of employees
Carlisle	Barwick Bros.	100	Carlisle	Linton Tweeds	90
	Bendall	100		Millican	70
	Border TV	83		Niven	50
	BRB Trust Estate			Otterburn Mill	100
	Management Scheme	1005		Pallinson Peat	9
	Engineering	60		Penguin Confectionery	350
	Carrs Biscuits	1550		Porter Engineering	60
	Cavagham & Grey	400		Pratchell	200
	Coulthard	150		Reid Bros	160
	Cowen Sheldon	300		Richardson Moss Litter	90
	Cowen	50		Robertson	200
	Dinky Wear	35		Robeson Border	
	Eden Construction	225		Transport	175
	Ready Mix Concrete	30		Teescott	200
	Eskimo Manufacturing	80		Securier	100
	Ferguson Bros	800		Simonacco	130
	Glen Eden Textiles	255		McAlpine	320
	Hackney	220		Stenhouse Northern	
	Harradine	350		Todd	100
	J. K. Innes	100		Watt	90
	Kangol Helmets	100		Sundar Fabrics	142
	Kangol Magnet	250			

An extract from a Kompass *directory.*

VI Perception of a local environment†

This unit was originally devised by Rex Walford of Maria Grey College of Education, Twickenham, in connection with a course for the training of junior/secondary teachers in geography and later used by fourth- and fifth-year (fourteen- to sixteen-year-olds) classes. It is designed to be a simple exercise in revealing different perceptions of a local environment, in relation to the size and extent of a particular neighbourhood. Since the idea of place is central to geography, the fact that people mean many different things when they refer to a particular place is an important concept to establish at some stage in a pupil's understanding of geography.

The material below is a description of the unit, plus the questionnaire used. The

†Rex Walford

questionnaire and map were devised in the first of the lessons of the unit, with the teacher and pupils together noting suitable landmarks that might help people to get their bearings when looking at a map of their local neighbourhood. In this lesson the teacher also considered with the class what would be the best kind of sample to use in investigating the perception of local inhabitants. There was also discussion and instruction about the way in which possible interviewees should and should not be approached.

Following this, members of the class 'administered' the questionnaire as part of their homework tasks. The second lesson in the unit was taken up with the correlation of questionnaire answers on to a 'master map' and with the analysis of the total response and of sub-groups. A third lesson was concerned with discussion of the results and some more general considerations about the way people perceived not only their own local environment, but also national and international ones.

Perception of a local environment

Lesson 1: The teacher introduced the exercise by asking the class to write down 'how you know when you are out of London'; the confusion of answers ('When the street lights stop,' 'When the buildings give way to open country,' 'When you don't see any more red buses,') typified the point that different places meant different things to different people. Was it easier to work out your own local environment? The class thought that it was, and said that there would be no trouble in delimiting their own neighbourhoods. Isleworth was chosen as a local example, and an overhead projector transparency made from the local 6″ map put on the screen. Class and teacher discussed what were the possible limits of the area.

Then the idea of a survey was introduced. The need to keep the survey simple was stressed and the class's aid was enlisted in deciding the exact nature of the questions to be asked. Class and teacher together constructed a skeleton map of the district with some basic landmarks on it, and agreed that people in the survey should be asked to 'draw a line around what they thought was Isleworth'. The teacher stressed that the map had to be as helpful as possible, since it was not people's map appreciation that was being tested, but their genuine perception; thus, if respondents found that they did not know how to start drawing the line, the questioner should help them on, by using a pencil himself and saying, 'Do you think Isleworth goes right down to the Chertsey Road?' etc.

The class then considered what factors might affect a person's answer. Some felt that the longer that you had lived in the place, the better you knew it, and so a question was asked about 'length of residence'. It was also felt that 'locals' would know better than strangers, and so a question was asked to distinguish these two types. The teacher then suggested that age might have something to do with the answer (since he was mindful of the fact that a once-flourishing minor regional centre was now in decline); it was decided therefore to poll a reasonable sample of three age-groups – fellow-school pupils, 'mums and dads and people of similar age', and old-age pensioners. (This rough grouping sorted out age-categories by sight, and thus avoided the need for a tricky question.)

The teacher explained what a reasonable sample might be, and the class agreed they would each be responsible for questioning six people – this would bring in a total of seventy respondents in each class. There was further discussion concerning how you did and did not ask questions of people, and of the need to be polite and well-mannered at all times when dealing with the general public. (Much of the questionnaire, however, was done in the school itself, and through parents, family and friends.) The teacher duplicated the map and questions later that day, and distributed eight copies to each pupil for their survey homework.

Lesson 2: The class assembled a few days later with most of the questionnaires completed as required. Some who had failed to get six respondents were made up for by enthusiasts who had done more than their fair share. The need for corporate effort to get results was again stressed. The problems of correlating the information were considerable, but were organized as follows. The survey papers were divided up into the three age groupings and then given to survey report teams (of about eight people each). The report teams noted down the answers to the questions, and also compared the maps of each respondent. They made comparison by noting which landmarks were inside and outside the boundary lines, rather than by trying to fit lines together by eye. They were asked to report (a) a 'mode' boundary line on one survey sheet, (b) a 'maximum and minimum' set of lines on another survey sheet, (c) any 'peculiarities' on yet another. While they did this another group assisted the teacher in preparing a master map for display, and a fifth group looked up present and past administrative boundaries of the area and other local descriptions in literature. Towards the end of this (somewhat informal) lesson, it became possible to transfer the generalized results of the survey teams on to the master map.

Lesson 3: There was time between lessons 2 and 3 for the teacher to tidy up any of the material which had not been properly sorted by the survey teams. Thus at the start of this lesson, he used both the original transparency, and the large master map to show the results of the survey. He had prepared overlays for the transparency, and these when laid on in order showed interestingly that the oldest age-group had the widest perception of Isleworth, and the youngest age-group (school-children) the smallest (when the generalized lines were drawn). Reasons for this were discussed, and the present perception of the place as 'in decline' advanced for the 'small' answer. Discussion then centred round some of the other problems originally raised, and the question of whether it made any difference if you lived in the area was discussed enthusiastically. One person in the class raised the problem of the large number of 'don't know's' in the survey and asked if they affected the result. It was agreed that they probably did, and that it might have been better to represent their imperfect knowledge by something other than a line. Then, the whole

31

question of drawing lines came under fire, and one member of the class suggested that the survey might have been simplified if respondents had simply been asked, 'Is *x* in Isleworth?' 'Is *y* in Isleworth' and so on. Many agreed that this would have made the survey easier.

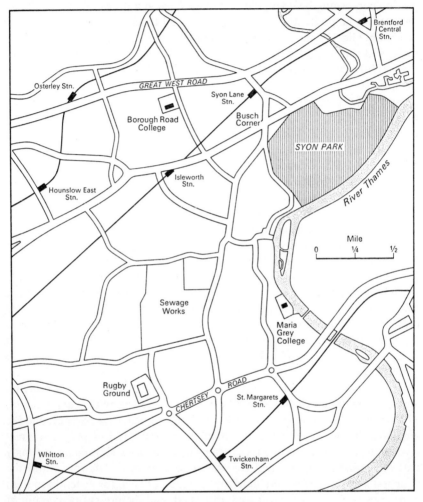

Fig 10. Isleworth: map for perception questionnaire

The discussion led back to 'what is London?' and the teacher spoke of commuters who now came from such places as Ramsgate and Brighton and who worked in the City. Were these Londoners now? The whole question of the 'world city' arose, and of the way in which distances and perceptions of places were altered by television and fast communication.

Questions to accompany map.(see fig. 10)
1 Draw a line around Isleworth (i.e. include within the line all the areas that you think are part of Isleworth).

   *If respondent does not feel able to do this because of lack of map ability, interviewer should try to complete map by using a question technique – 'Is it still Isleworth the other side of the Chertsey Road?' 'Does Isleworth stretch up to Busch Corner?' etc.
2 How long have you lived in Isleworth?
3 If you do not live in Isleworth, which district do you live in?
4 Put an X on the map where you live, if it is within the area shown.

VII A fresh approach to glaciation†

This unit was devised by C. J. S. Colthurst of Lancing College, Sussex, and used in a Europe course with fourth-year (fourteen- to fifteen-year-old) pupils. It was devised in order to develop an investigational approach to glaciation (rather than the more usual descriptive one) and to develop simple quantitative techniques. The simple forms of measurement proposed were used to make deductions about the nature and behaviour of ice.

The class are given Swiss maps to work from (in this unit, the 1 : 50,000 map of the Sustenpass was used), and groups of four or five pupils can work from one large map. Each person in a group is asked to carry out a series of measurements on the glacier given to them. The data sheet from which they work is reproduced below, and also the question given to them for written answers.

The first lesson of the unit was taken for explanation of the task, and for the drawing of catchment areas, and the subsequent measurements required. The individual written answers to questions were begun at the end of this lesson and finished for homework. In the second lesson of the unit, there was discussion in groups about the answers written up by individuals. Then followed class discussion and the comments of the teacher. In a third lesson, the conclusions drawn from lesson 2 were applied to another glaciated area, and tested in the same way.

Instructions given to pupils for glaciation exercise
1 Look at the map that you have been given and identify the main glaciers on it.
2 Use tracing paper to show clearly the limits of the catchment basins and choose a suitable method for working out the area required. You will find that squared tracing paper or cellofilm will help.
3 Fill in the table below, in relation to each glacier that you are working on.

†C. J. S. Colthurst

Glacier measurements	Trift	Stein	Rhone	Damma
(a) Area of snow and ice				
(b) Total area of catchment basin				
(c) Height of snout				
(d) Approx. height of snowline				
(e) Approx. gradient of snow				
(f) Approx. highest point of snow/ice cover				
(g) Approx. average height of snow and ice				
(h) Orientation of glacier (NNE, SW, etc.)				

The table will be completed at the end of the lesson

4 Answer the questions below in your notebook. We shall use these questions as the basis for discussion in the next lesson.

i What other measurements would you like to know to explain the differences between the glaciers?

ii What do you think is the depth of snow in different places?

iii Where does the depth of snow and ice vary? Why?

iv What is different about the areas where there are frequent 'blue cracks' in the ice?

v Study the areas of bare rock exposed above the snow. Where do they mainly occur?

VIII A role-playing exercise about town development and water resources†

This lesson unit was devised by Margaret Caistor and other members of the General Studies Team, whilst at Hove County Grammar School. It was used by pupils in the lower-sixth form (sixteen- to seventeen-year-olds) as the culminating exercise in a general studies course, with the theme, man and his physical environment. In this case, water was being used as an example of a physical resource in the course, and pupils had already had lectures on water supply and shortage in Britain, and on water pollution. They had completed work on directed topics and visited the local river authority. The Chayton role-play was designed to bring out the conflicting demands for water in Britain, and the possibility of alternative decisions concerning its use. It was also designed to test verbal, rather than written, ability in the course.

The accompanying two data sheets, reproduced below, were given to each participant, and in addition one role (see specimen example) was assigned to each pair of students. The teacher, role-playing the ministry representative from London, opened the first lesson, and spoke briefly about the general situation as outlined on the data sheets. An overhead projector transparency map of the mythical Chayton area was

†Margaret Caistor

used to develop the situation. Then followed ten to fifteen minutes in which the data sheets were examined by the participants. They were encouraged to write some introductory notes on their attitude to the proposed development. (The teacher's help was needed here – in some cases to prompt with relevant questions, and in other cases to give encouragement to shy pupils who had not experienced role-play before.) Then followed an open town meeting with the chairman calling on individuals to state their points of view. This went on through a double period, with open discussion and argument following the original opening statements. Finally a vote was taken about the proposed expansion.

At Hove, the exercise was played simultaneously by six different groups, and a 'fascinating variation' in attitude was reported. The exercise was felt to be very successful both by the pupils at the time and by staff in evaluating the course.

The data used in the exercise was from material already gathered from local river boards, and from the local planning authority.

(Data sheet 1)

Data relating to the future development of Chayton (*with special reference to water supply*)
(Prepared for a committee of all interested parties convened in October 1969)

Members of the committee
  1 Chairman, ministry representative from London
  2 Member of the Minshire River Authority, Mr J. Sherwood
  3 Chayton New Town Development Corporation planner, Mr. T Matthews
  4 Chayton New Town Development Corporation engineer, Mr L. Carter
  5 Councillor, Chayton UDC, Mr I. Ingham (Lab.)
  6 Councillor, Minshire RDC, Mr T. Webb (Con.)
  7 Sir John Coldean (very large landowner)
  8 Owner of Chayton Dye Works, Mr S. Ingham
  9 Director of Chayton Steel Company, Mr P Steel
10 NFU representative, Mr L. Field, B.Sc., Agric.
11 Local Naturalist Society representative, Miss E. Jenkins
12 Local Chamber of Commerce representative, Mr W. Smith
13 Chairman of Chayton Ratepayers Association, Mrs T. Good
14 Private developer interested in marina, Mr G. Bloom
15 Director of Minshire Water Board, Mr P. Watson, Dip. Pub. Health

Information on Chayton
Chayton is a town of 50,000 pop., with two industries, a steel-works and a dye-works. It is also the local market town, attracts some retired residents and is the social focus of the neighbouring countryside. This area of the Minshire RDC is mainly good agricultural land although as precipitation is marginal, supplementary irrigation is needed in summer months. The farming population is prosperous and takes an active interest in the affairs of Chayton.

(Data sheet 2)

Data on water supply in Chayton area

	Estimated cost of water		Estimated situation			Estimated use of water			Estimated cost of water		
	Unpurified	Purified	Popu-lation	Industry	Agri-culture	Popu-lation	Industry	Agri-culture	Popu-lation	Industry	Agri-culture
A 1969	£200 m g d 20p th g d	£300 m g d 30p th g d	100,000	steel co. dye-works (20 galls each)	spray irrigation	2 m g d	10 m g d	½ m g d	£600 p d water rate 1·5p	£2000 p d	£100 p d
B 1979 (minimal expansion)	£225 m g d (12% incr)	£375 m g d (25% incr)	120,000	steel co. dye-works both expanded	spray irrigation expanded	2·4 m g d	15 m g d	¾ m g d	£900 p d water rate 1·8p	£3375 p d	£168·75 p d
C 1979 (maximum expansion)	£281 m g d (40% incr)	£412 m g d (37% incr)	170,000	steel co. dye-works both expanded and new light industry	spray irrigation expanded as B	3·4 m g d	20 m g d	¾ m g d	£1400·8 p d water rate 2p	£5620 p d (steel and dye) £4215	£210·75 p d

m – million   th – thousand   g – gallons   d – day

The town itself is situated at the confluence of the two streams which form the River Dube. The main tributary rises in the area of high ground moors and open country, some thirty miles from Chayton. This river supplies some rural water supply and agricultural demand before it reaches Chayton where it is used for domestic and industrial purposes. The dye-works and domestic demand are taken off before the confluence; but the steel-works abstracts water just below this point. Below the town the river flows through an attractive parkland area and some ten miles of its left bank are owned by the large landowner Sir John Coldean. The right bank was used in this area by the local fishing association which had to move upstream above the town because of pollution about five years ago.

Into the Chayton area the government plan to move part of the East End London overspill in a New Town of 50,000. There will be some development of light industry. After some preliminary cost analysis and surveying the government has sent a representative to form a committee of interested parties.

Data concerning use of water in the Chayton area

1 There are three users of water: industry; agriculture; domestic.
2 There are two types of water: purified; unpurified.
  Each type has a different rate of charges. This differential will be influenced by the type of expansion.
3 At the moment there is sufficient water.
4 Without the new town the rivers and occasional bore holes would satisfy demand in 1979.
5 If the new town is built new water supplies will be needed and a reservoir scheme is favoured by the government. They would subsidize the cost on condition users of water in the area observed strict pollution laws.

A sample role sheet (given to pupils)

Development of Chayton 1969–79
You are the Chayton Development Corporation planner, Timothy Matthews, Ph.D.
You are twenty-nine years old, have a first degree in geography and a Ph.D. in urban geography. You are single, ambitious and not a native of this part of the country. You are intolerant of muddle and believe that tact is of little value. You have helped on the Cwmbran Development Corporation in Wales, and are anxious to bring a New Town into existence, yourself as chief planner.
Introductory notes on the scheme..
Notes on the meeting..

(1 page allowed for each of these)

IX Testing explanations of city structure†

This unit was devised by John Rolfe of Haberdashers' Aske's School, Elstree, and used in a first year sixth-form (sixteen- to seventeen-year-olds) course on urban geography.

The unit was designed to introduce pupils to some theories of city structure (Burgess, Hoyt, Harris and Ullman – see Mayer and Kohn, *Readings in Urban Geography*, University of Chicago Press, 1966) and to relate these to work done in the field. Pupils were presumed to have an introduction to the recording of land use in towns earlier in their school career. The material below is a description of the unit, which lasted a total of four forty-minute periods. In the first two periods (a double-period), pupils went to St Albans and carried out land-use mapping tasks along selected transect routes within the town. (This work overlapped beyond the end of school time.) In the third period, groups of pupils compiled a large map of St Albans in land-use zones, and then compared these with various models of city structure introduced by the teacher. The fourth period was taken up with the assessment of relationships and subsequent discussion.

The structure of a town

1 In addition to its value as a *basis* for urban research and planning, the general land-use map is a graphic presentation of a challenge. Raymond E. Murphy, *The American City*, 1966, p. 207.

Emphasizing the idea of a basis, the first step was to familiarize the students with mapping land use in a town and incidentally in getting to know the town better. With so much work already done by A. E. Smailes, our local town of St Albans was an obvious choice as our example. The students were split up into groups and they literally compared Smailes' map (fig. 11, *Geography of Towns*) with the present-day land use overall, noting any alterations. Suitable maps were obtained free of charge from a local estate agent. (NB The exercise can, of course, be done using only the map compiled in the field.)

2 Back in the classroom, a fair copy of the land-use map of St Albans was compiled. Time permitting, it would have been preferable to study one or two other towns at least, e.g. Watford or Rickmansworth, so that comparisons could have been made. This brought us on to the next point.

3 'Is there to some degree a common pattern or order which carries over from city to city which implies similar processes of origin?' Murphy, *op. cit.*, p. 207.

†John Rolfe

4 The concentric zone theory (E. W. Burgess)

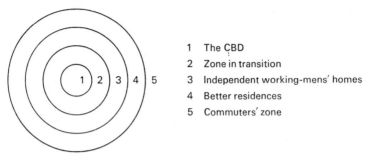

1 The CBD
2 Zone in transition
3 Independent working-mens' homes
4 Better residences
5 Commuters' zone

Fig 11. The concentric zone theory of city structure (after E. W. Burgess)

This theory was then presented (using Murphy, or Johnson's *Urban Geography*, Pergamon, 1966) and then tested against the 'model' of Smailes' map of St Albans, by superimposing Burgess' annular rings on tracing paper over the St Albans map. (Cello-film on the overhead projector could be used equally well.) When acceptable boundaries had been agreed, based on the Burgess classifications, a fair copy was drawn. A discussion was then based on comparing the two. Although some 'degree of fit' was seen, the Burgess map did not define essential variations too well.

5 The sector theory (Homer Hoyt)

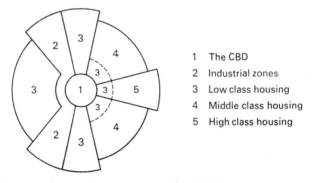

1 The CBD
2 Industrial zones
3 Low class housing
4 Middle class housing
5 High class housing

Fig 12. The sector theory of city structure (after H. Hoyt)

Hoyt's sector theory was then advanced, and fitted to St Albans in a similar way. Although figures of rents had not been available to us at this stage (rateable values would be an alternative) subjective comparisons suggested that Hoyt's was not a very good zonal model for St Albans.

6 The multiple nuclei concept (Harris and Ullman)

Harris and Ullman's multiple nuclei concept (a combination of the previous two) was then explained, and the zones fitted to St Albans as before. In the discussion which followed it was agreed that while being the nearer to Smailes' (which it must be remembered is being used as the model) some anomalies were noted.

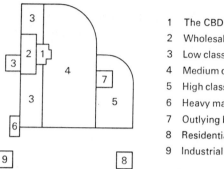

1   The CBD
2   Wholesale
3   Low class residential
4   Medium class residential
5   High class residential
6   Heavy manufacturing
7   Outlying business district
8   Residential suburbs
9   Industrial suburbs

Fig 13. The multiple nuclei theory of city structure (after Harris and Ullman)

7 Finally, Mann's structure of a hypothetical British city (see Johnson, *op. cit.*, p. 169) was drawn up and compared. It was agreed that this was the one generalized model that appeared to fit St Albans best.

Conclusions
1 St Albans (or any local town?) was fairly familiar to the students and a useful basis for discussing models and reality.
2 Worthwhile zonal concepts of city structure had been taught.

X The interpretation of land use patterns†

This unit was devised by R. J. Robinson of City of Birmingham College of Education and has been used successfully both on field courses and in the classroom with sixth-form (seventeen- to eighteen-year-old) students.

It is designed to use the maps of the Second Land Use Survey for close analysis, and to go beyond the method of verbal description of comparison between land use and relief maps, geological maps, etc. Such comparison is often visual, sometimes with overlays, but is certainly subjective and liable to include undetected errors. The unit reproduced here uses the techniques of random sampling (either for work in the field or in the classroom) for analysis. The results of random sampling can be analysed through dispersion diagrams, or scatter diagrams and matrices.

The material that follows is a description of how to develop random samples from

Land Use Maps, and how to test for error in the random sample before further analysis takes place. Land Use Maps are available for some parts of the country, and cost (usually) 75p each. They are obtainable from Dr A. Coleman, the Director of the Second Land Use Survey, Department of Geography, Kings College, Strand, London, W.C.2.

The interpretation of land use patterns

Point sampling is preferred to line sampling or area sampling (quadrat sampling) in rural areas for several reasons. Firstly the information gathered by point sampling can be analysed without further processing. The characteristics found at a point may be described simply, thus 'grassland', 'alluvium', 'slope 2°', 'soil pH 6', etc. On the other hand data from a line or quadrat sample leaves the investigator with many problems; a line might be '25% grassland', '40% alluvium', 'slope', 'soil'. One might have to sample the sample line to establish exact relationships. Secondly, as shown later, the calculation of the significance of point sample results is arithmetically simple. Thirdly, as again shown later, simple analytical techniques can be readily applied to point sample results. Fourthly, the collection of point data is much more of a practical proposition in the field than line or quadrat.

The sampling must contain a random element to justify the application of statistical tests to the sample results.

The disadvantage of this sampling method, and perhaps almost any other objective approach, is the time involved. For worthwhile results a total of a hundred sample points should be the aim. In the field, with points spread over a square mile area, two people can very comfortably visit fifteen points in a day. Thus clearly such work has to be a combined operation, with result tables drawn up to include several people's work. In the classroom using maps two people should be able to extract data for about twenty-five points in an hour. Again results should be combined. Speeds of course increase with experience.

The work can be divided into three parts: preparation, collection of information, analysis of information.

The preparation involves the selection of the area to be studied. Any accessible rural area with a variety of land use could be studied in the field; for classroom exercise the northern part of Sheet 454 (Nuneaton) of the $2\frac{1}{2}''$ Land Use Map has proved satisfactory. At this stage decisions should be made about the hypotheses to be tested. The view that field work and investigation should test hypotheses rather than merely describe patterns is developed by J. A. Everson in *Geography,* January 1969. Usually work on rural land use will consider hypotheses concerned with the relationships between land-use patterns and some aspects of the physical environment such as altitude, slope, soil type and structure, and geology. Increasing stress has also been laid on the relation of land use to distance from farm, village, road or track.

The next step in the preparation is the construction of a grid covering the map of the area to be studied in order to generate the required number of random points. The best all-purpose grid is a straightforward 10 × 10 square grid to cover the area. It is possible to use a random number table (S. Gregory, *Statistical Methods and the Geographer*, page 101) to generate points by taking the numbers in groups of four in sequence. This can be used as four figure references to locate points on the 10 × 10 grid. Thus if the first eight figures in the random number table were '42670632', the first two points would be 4267 and 0632 as shown on the grid below:

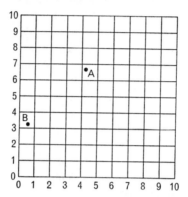

Fig 14. Grid for random number point generation

The number of points generated will depend on the accuracy of the results required. It is worth noting some further points with reference to the grid. The straightforward random sample may be considered unsatisfactory for some studies. In this case a modification may be attempted. For example if the influence of one factor in particular were being studied it might be possible to stratify the random sample. A study might attempt to test only the relationship between land use and distance from a village, and instead of a square grid it might be desirable to use circles concentric on the village at say quarter-mile intervals. The distance rings could then be sampled separately to ensure an adequate number of sample points for each ring. Similarly if an area were clearly divided according to altitude or geology it would be possible to sample each sub-region separately.

When the random points have been generated onto the map and the problem to be studied has been clearly outlined, the way is open to complete an outline data sheet.

This is the next stage – collection of information. In the field there is of course no need to survey the entire land use of the area. Instead each random point is visited and the relevant information noted. This information would probably include altitude, slope (measured with a home-made clinometer), soil type, depth and structure, aspect, geology, distance to nearest track, farm or village. In the classroom exercise the data which will have to be extracted from maps will certainly exclude soil characteristics and perhaps slope. At each observation point the land use is also noted. This is probably best done on the basis of the classification provided for the Second Land Utilization Survey. It may be economical to combine some categories, but the use of this classification has the added advantage that field results can be compared with published maps.

Data table for random point sample.

Point (Grid Reference)	Land use	Drift geology	Altitude (in ft)	Slope (angle)	Topsoil depth (inches)	pH	% Clay	Other observations (e.g. animals, improvements)

The final major stage is the presentation and analysis of the results. Before attempting any analysis in detail it is necessary to test for error in the random sample. Most of what follows will be found in detail in S. Gregory, *Statistical Methods and the Geographer*, but it may be worthwhile showing how these techniques apply to this specific type of work.

Presentation and analysis of random point sample results
It is vital to know how significant the results are. Suppose that in a random point sample of 300 points the land use results were:

Woodland 30 points
Arable 120 points
Grass 150 points

The sample thus suggests that the area under study is 10% woodland, 40% arable and 50% grass. Is this result likely to be accurate? First calculate the Standard Error for each % using the formula:

$$\text{S.E.} = \sqrt{\frac{p\% \times q\%}{n}}$$

where n is the number of random points, p% is the % we are interested in, and q% is $100 - p\%$ (i.e. all the rest). Thus the S.E. for woodland in this example is:

$$\sqrt{\frac{10 \times 90}{300}} = \sqrt{\frac{9}{3}} = \sqrt{3} = 1\cdot73$$

The Standard Error is then used to show the probable limits of sample error. There is a 68% chance that the true % will be within 1 S.E. of the sample results; there is a 95% chance that it will be within 2 S.E. of the sample result; there is a 99·7% probability that the true % will be within 3 S.E. of the sample

result. In the example above we may say from the sample that the % of woodland in the area is between 8·3% and 11·7% at the 68% probability level or
between 6·5% and 13·5% at the 95% probability level. Geographers often
work at the 95% probability level.

Graphing results

The % of different types of land use in the example above could be shown
with the appropriate Standard Errors:

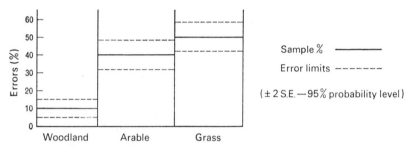

Fig 15. Sample results graphed, with standard error shown

Dispersion diagrams

The relation between various factors (for example land use and angle of slope)
can be assessed with the help of dispersion diagrams. Median and quartile
lines are helpful in the interpretation of dispersion diagrams. The median is
the line at the mid-point of the scatter – if there were 17 points the 9th would
be on the median. The quartiles separate the upper and lower halves into
halves again – thus with 17 points the quartiles would be at the 5th and 13th
points:

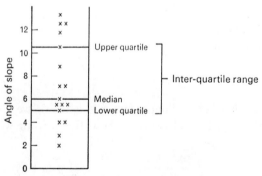

Fig 16. Dispersion diagram showing angles of slope for a 17-point sample

Comparison of dispersion diagrams

The relationship between a variable (for example angle of slope) and other
features sampled (for example land use distribution) can be assessed. In the

diagram below various categories of land use are plotted against angle of slope, each point representing a random sample point.

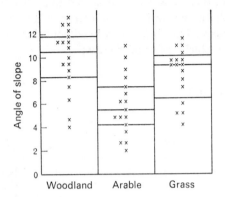

Fig 17. Land use graphed against angle of slope

The median and quartiles are plotted for each column.
When comparing any two columns there are three possibilities:

i   the quartiles do not overlap at all – arable and woodland above – which would mean that angle of slope was significantly related to this distribution of woodland compared to arable.

ii the quartiles only overlap – arable and grassland above – which suggests that angle of slope is probably significantly related to the distribution of arable compared to grassland.

iii any other overlap – grass and woodland – no significant relationship.

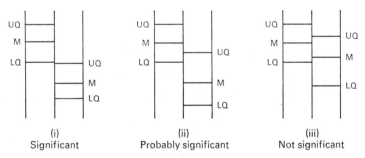

Fig 18. Comparison of dispersion diagrams for significance

Scatter diagrams

If the data for two variables is quantitative (i.e. measured in numbers or ranks) a scatter diagram could be used to show their relationship – for example altitude (in feet) compared to angle of slope (in degrees) at each random point.

Matrices

A matrix may be useful to compare two variables (for example land use and surface geology) neither of which is measured quantitively. The number of random points with the appropriate combination of land usage and geology is entered in each square. Thus below in a hypothetical example, there were 21 points on alluvium which were under grass:

Matrix 1 (observed data)

Surface geology

	1	2	3	4	5	Total	Surface Geology Key:
Woodland	5	0	0	11	4	20	1 Bagshot beds
Arable	1	33	18	2	6	60	2 Chalk
Grassland	3	20	9	16	21	69	3 Upper greensand
Heathland	48	0	2	1	0	51	4 Clay
							5 Alluvium
Total	57	53	29	30	31	200	

This matrix may be considered in two ways – either starting from each type of land use (reading across the rows), or starting from each type of surface geology (reading down the columns). First look at the rows, and consider the distribution of arable. Sixty of the 200 sample points were classified as arable, thus 60/200 of the sample is arable. If arable was associated equally with each type of surface geology it would be reasonable to assume that 60/200 of each type of surface geology would be arable. Look at the columns and consider column 2 – Chalk. 53 of the 200 sample points fell on chalk. If chalk had an average proportion of arable on its surface we would find that 60/200 of the 53 points were arable –

i.e. $53 \times 60/200 = 16$ approx. (these calculations take little time if a slide rule is used).

A calculation like this can be made for each box in the matrix and a new matrix (matrix 2) produced which shows the situation as it would be if each type of surface geology had a fair share, or average quota, of each type of land use in the area.

Compare matrix 1 with matrix 2 and associations between certain types of land use and certain types of geology are quickly spotted. For example instead of 16 arable points on chalk there are 33 – twice as many as expected by the average calculation. A useful way to tabulate these associations for study or comparison between areas is to divide the actual number of points (matrix 1) by the expected or average number of points (matrix 2), and use the answers to complete a third matrix (matrix 3).

Thus for arable on chalk:

$$\frac{\text{observed number}}{\text{expected number}} = \frac{33}{16} = 2 \cdot 06$$

Grassland on bagshot beds would be worked out thus:

Grassland   69 out of 200 points
Bagshot beds 57 out of 200 points

so average expected is that 69/200 of the bagshot beds will be grassland

or $57 \times 69/200 = 20$ points approx. (entered on matrix 2)

However, matrix 1 shows that only 3 grassland points were located on the bagshot beds, so

$$\frac{\text{observed number}}{\text{expected number}} = \frac{3}{20} = 0 \cdot 15 \text{ (entered on matrix 3)}$$

Thus on matrix 3 1·0 indicates an expected average share,
  more than 1·0 suggests a positive association between the land use and geology concerned,
  less than 1·0 suggests a negative relationship.

Matrix 2 (expected distribution)

Surface geology

	1	2	3	4	5	Total
W.	6	5	3	3	3	20
A.	17	16	9	9	9	60
G.	20	18	10	10	11	69
H.	14	14	7	8	8	51
Total	57	53	29	30	31	200

Matrix 3 $\left(\dfrac{\text{observed}}{\text{expected}}\right)$

Surface geology

	1	2	3	4	5
W.	0·8	0	0	3·6	1·3
A.	0·1	2·1	2·0	0·2	0·7
G.	0·2	1·1	0·9	1·6	1·9
H.	3·4	0	0·3	0·1	0

Matrix 3 may now be read in terms of rows or columns. The grassland row shows that grassland is particularly associated with surface geologies 4 (clay) and 5 (alluvium), but a very low proportion is found on 1 (bagshot beds). An average amount is found on 2 and 3. Column 2 (chalk) for instance suggests a very strong association with arable, an average amount of grassland, but very little or no heath and woodland in this area judging by this sample. The analysis of the data by some or all of these methods can often be accomplished by group work, and fruitful discussion may follow. The analysis should pinpoint relationships, but of course like all statistical analysis cannot explain the relationships. The work so far provides an objective basis upon which to base interpretations, and has given the pupil the opportunity of obtaining and analysing objectively evidence relating to rural land use patterns.

XI Towards a structured investigation of rural environment†

An increasing interest in the theories and ideas underlying the spatial organization of the environment has not decreased interest in field work – rather the reverse. The two final units in the section (XI and XII) represent approaches to field work which are coloured by recent developments, and though they deal respectively with rural and urban work, they have a good deal in common with each other.

Vincent Tidswell, in this unit, after a brief introduction offers a clear structure of the way in which such work can be done. It is significant that he suggests no less than three distinct stages in work before pupils go out into the field; all three are essential parts of the unit.

The work begins with preliminary consideration of what is being attempted – a definition of aims. Then follows an examination of data and a comparison of this with some general measures of e.g. rural settlement spacing, threshold populations for types of shops. Then, combining what has been learnt from the first two stages, comes the formulation of hypotheses – ideas to test in the field. This, if done by discussion methods in the classroom, not only effectively reinforces work already done, but stimulates interest and challenge in the field work itself.

Stage four, going into the field, is done with the hypotheses in mind. The environment is looked at selectively rather than comprehensively, and proponents of this style of field work would argue that it thus becomes a more realistic task for pupils, as well as encouraging a greater depth of thought and observation. Stage five represents the spin-off from this. Besides the recording and display of the data in tables and maps, there is consideration of the hypotheses (ideas/questions/hunches) again and discussion about them. Are they likely to apply equally well in other places? What modifications are needed to the original statements? And so on.

The scheme of work suggested here is intended as an exercise for senior pupils, and the testing of hypotheses consequently demands some ordered thinking. However, a judicious reduction in the number of hypotheses tested and a selection of those

†W. V. Tidswell

chosen for study should enable such an investigative approach to be pursued from the age of eleven or twelve upwards.

The explosive advent of model theory and quantitative techniques offers exciting new suggestions for themes relevant to a structured discipline and a methodology worthy of the name 'scientific method of enquiry'. The conceptual thinking embodied in models provides a structure within which it is possible to isolate the problem (see spheres of influence, p. 51–3). Newer techniques (sampling) mean swift collection of more accurate data which may be statistically evaluated, and hence lead to a more penetrating analysis. The problem solving approach to field work helps eliminate 'noise' and concentration restricts the collection of data to that which is relevant and which may be fully interpreted. Integration of field work with course work is entirely natural since the problems investigated arise from the latter in a spontaneous manner. Furthermore, although for practical reasons actual investigations must be of an individual nature, provided they are correctly structured, valid generalizations may be made from the results.

Characteristics of this approach may be summarized as:

1 Scientific method of enquiry inculcates logical and accurate investigation, data processing and sound deduction.
2 There is spontaneous integration within the theoretical framework of the discipline.
3 Imperative definition of the problem minimizes data collection and the emphasis on data processing ensures maximum results.
4 Field investigation may be carried out in nondescript areas and is not confined to spectacular dramatic landscapes.

It is hoped such an approach not only represents a progression in field-work methodology, but also forms an integral part of the current trend to move away from the circumscribed idiographic study towards a more acceptable nomothetic one and from a man/land analysis of environment towards the concept of a man/man relationship. An example follows.

Village studies
Many field-work centres are themselves located in rural areas and in any event the study of a village usually forms an integral part of a field-work programme. The variety of themes which present themselves for investigation is clearly indicated by H. D. Clout's diagram: (see page 50).

It shows the impossibility of handling total landscape and the urgent need for selectivity in structuring field research. The focal point of fig. 19 is seen to be settlement and occupance which interact with all other elements. For this reason settlement is the theme selected as the most rewarding study in the limited time usually available.

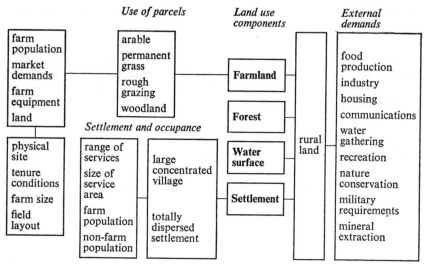

Fig 19. *Some components of country planning studies (from H. D. Clout in* Trends in Geography, *ed. R. U. Cooke and J. H. Johnson, Pergamon).*

Normally in planning a programme of work one is involved with a large group of students or sixth formers. Since they are subdivided into smaller groups to study one particular village, the number of settlements visited may be large. Modern methodology in the form of random sampling or stratified random sampling[1]* enables the total number of units of investigation to be selected so that results may be evaluated in a statistical way, and valid substantiated generalizations made about the study area as a whole. This latter step is especially important in testing theoretical concepts of the discipline discussed in classwork.

Units for investigation are selected in a random way by numbering all the villages and calling random numbers. If a classified selection is needed e.g. half the number to be on chalk and half to be on clay, then these categories must be numbered separately. Full details for this procedure and the evaluation of the sampling error are contained in Cole and King, *Quantitative Geography,* Ch. 3. See also Unit X in this book.

Stage one in any field research is the isolation of the problem, which should be clarified into an articulate statement of aims. These may be defined as:

1 Examination of the geometry of settlement patterns within the study area[2]
2 Consideration of the effects of increasing distance from the urban centre in terms of growth, decline and provision of amenity
3 Evaluation of chance factors *vis-à-vis* rational elements in siting and development of settlements
4 Discovery of pattern of retail trading in relation to breaking point theory and range of a good[3]

* Figures in square brackets indicate references on page 56.

5 Testing of and perhaps revision of threshold figures[4] (See tables below.)
6 Establishing *raison d'être* of village – realization that village cannot be regarded as an inward looking self-contained unit in terms of food, work or entertainment.

Stage two is the examination of such data as is already available for the study area as a whole and for selected villages within it. This should include the preparation of base maps and visits to secondary sources.

For the study area as a whole
1 Using topographical maps:

    (a) determine relief index[5]
    (b) count total number of villages
    (c) determine mean distance separating villages
    Compare these results with the data provided (spacing of settlements) and note any similarity or marked deviation.

Spacing of rural settlements in differing physical landscapes

Area (400 sq. km)	Number of villages	Mean distance apart (miles)	Relief Index
Burton on Trent	50	1·14	1·0
Fen Margin	54	1·30	4·5
Herefordshire	45	1·08	8·66
Vale of Pickering	45	1·10	9·30
South Downs	44	1·10	17·00
Black Mountains	35	1·09	34·00
Snowdonia	23	1·10	55·30
Lake District	16	2·10	64·3

2 Use population census and determine population size of urban areas – are they all of the same order? The Population Census (County Report) is available in public libraries.
3 Prepare three traced overlay base maps and on each mark the urban areas with a square and the villages with a dot. On the first overlay draw circles at x miles radii from the urban centre/centres.
4 On the second overlay draw in significant physical/geological boundaries e.g. fen, chalk, sandstone.
5 On the third overlay simulate urban spheres of influence using Reilly's Law of Retail Gravitation[6] (See fig. 20.)
6 Select villages for study by stratified random samples on the basis of
    (a) distance zones
    (b) physical divisions.

7 Select villages for study in evaluating spheres of influence if not contained within random choice.

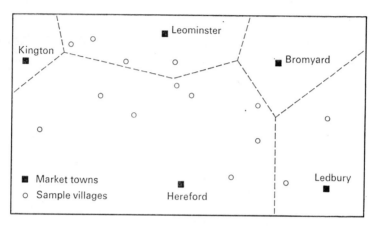

Fig 20. Spheres of influence for Herefordshire market towns simulated using Reilly's law of retail gravitation

For the group of selected villages
1 Visit libraries and record offices to establish population growth.
2 Visit planning office to ascertain details of planning permission and/or restriction.
3 Visit local estate agents to try and ascertain property values.

Some guidance about thresholds
1

Shop	Threshold	Shop	Threshold
Boots the Chemist	10,000	John Lewis	50,000 for
Mac Fisheries	25,000		supermarket
Barratts Shoes	20–30,000	John Lewis	100,000 for
Sainsbury Grocers	60,000		departmental
Marks and Spencers	50–100,000		store

Source: Chorley and Haggett, eds., *Frontiers in Geographical Teaching*, Methuen.

2 Threshold population for selected functions in South Ontario

Function	Threshold	Function	Threshold
General Food Stores	65	Lawyers	742
General Clothing	85	Dentists	1734
Banks	727	Opticians	2890

Source: Yeates, *An Introduction to Quantitative Analysis in Economic Geography*, p. 105.

3 Threshold populations in Snohomish County, Washington.

Function	Threshold	Function	Threshold
Filling Station	196	Chemist	458
Restaurant	276	Beautician	480
Tavern	282	Clothing	590
Doctor	380	Lawyer	528
Barber	386	Dry Cleaner	754
Dentist	426	Shoe Repairs	896
Fuel Merchant	453	Animal Feed Stores	526
Hardware	431	Farm Implement Dealer	650
Furniture	546	Veterinary Surgeon	579

Source: Extract from P. Ambrose, *Analytical Human Geography*, pp. 154–55, where a much fuller list may be found.

For each individual village
1 Examine the topographical maps for details of site:
(a) try to see, as Jean Mitchell suggests,[7] with the eye of the original settler – food, fuel, water, shelter and defence. An extract from the Domesday account of Marden may help you see with the eyes of the early settlers and to appreciate how they obtained the essentials for living:

The king holds Marden. There are several hides but of these only 2 pay geld. This land is divided among many men. In demesne the king has 3 ploughs and there are 25 villeins and 5 borders and 2 oxmen and 4 serfs and 4 coliberts. Among them all they have 21 ploughs. There is a mill worth 20s and 25 sticks of eels. The wood renders 20s. There is a fish pond which pays no rent. From the salt pans in Droitwich 9 loads of salt are paid or 9d.

(b) Is the physical site unique or not unique i.e. are there identical physical features close by without settlement present?
(c) look at present day needs in terms of:

i   shortest road distance to nearest town
ii distance to nearest A road
iii frequency of bus services (see timetables)
iv provision of amenities – golf, fishing, sailing, woodland.

2 Measure the shape of the village and the parish.[8]
3 Are complementary types of terrain present within the parish boundary e.g. floodplain and terrace; fen and chalk?
4 From population data state population today; growth or decline, date of significant change.
5 Using the electoral roll establish a random sample for socio-economic survey (see questionnaire at the end of this chapter) and re-arrange addresses on minimum itinerary basis. Electoral rolls are available in village post offices and county libraries.

6 With reference to threshold figures decide what amenities it is feasible to expect within the village.[9]

7 Complete summary pro-forma as far as possible.

8 Study all the data and together with your knowledge of underlying theory formulate hypotheses about expected patterns of phenomena.

Stage three is the formulation of hypotheses to guide work in the field. These will be derived from theoretical concepts taught in class and from the handling of existing data. At a more sophisticated level they will also contain heuristic elements. Some relevant examples to be tested may be:

1 Actual site bears little or no relationship to unique physical conditions. (If proven, then chance element plays significant part in precise location within broad physical limits. Compare with location of industry studies.)

2 There is no difference in spacing of settlements in chalk and fen areas.

3 There is a marked difference in parish shape between fen and chalk (historical geography and timing).

4 Growing villages are commuter villages and hence show greater accessibility to urban areas.

5 Within the zone of growth there is a strong chance element in location of actual growth points (speculative builders).

6 Numbers of growing villages decrease with increasing distance from urban centres.

7 Property values decrease with increasing distance from urban areas.

8 Provision of commercial amenity increases with distance from higher order settlements.

9 Reilly's law continues to play a significant part in predicting the pattern of retail trading in rural areas.

NB It is possible to re-cycle the testing of these hypotheses by revising the original distance zones.

Stage four is the work actually carried out in the field and may be summarized as:

1 On the 6″ base map mark with a red dot individual houses and with red hachuring all housing estates built since 1950. Locate all commercial premises: S = shop; P = pub; G = garage. NB School and post office already marked – check location for accuracy.

2 Carry out threshold test.

3 Carry out socio-economic survey.

NB No attempt is made to map the entire village in terms of age of building, function and building materials used. Data collection is restricted to that relevant to hypotheses to be tested.

4 Complete village pro-forma. Group leaders transfer to summary sheets for landscape types and/or distance zones. Examples of these are found at the end of the chapter.

Stage five consists of the interpretation and processing of data: hypothesis evaluation.

A. Map analysis

1 Is there any significant difference in density between types of landscape and/or distance zones?
2 Are commercial amenities centrally placed to attract maximum trade, e.g. shop in village centre, garage on principal through-route?
3 Is the new building related to (a) physical terrain (b) road network (c) neither? Group leaders transfer to summary sheets.

B. The data

Summary sheets for landscape types, distance zones and for testing retail trading areas may appear tedious in fact but they facilitate deductions. Some examples of the deductions to be made are:

Within a particular distance zone or landscape type
1 How many villages occupy unique sites?
2 In how many cases does growth relate to physical geography of site?
3 How many villages/parishes have a similar shape? Is there any relationship between shape of village and shape of parish?
4 What is the number of villages (a) growing (b) declining?
5 How many parishes have complementary terrains within their boundaries?
6 Do shopping habits reveal expected destination and the range of a good?

Between distance zones and landscape types
Comparisons may be made because of the standardized way in which data has been collected and recorded. The re-formulation of hypotheses and null hypotheses is also facilitated, together with evaluation of the original hypotheses. Since all units of investigation formed a sample the results may be evaluated as estimates of the characteristics for the area as a whole. Relationships between phenomena may be determined by rank correlation methods and/or graphs and/or regression analysis.[10]

It should certainly be possible to make valid and substantiated generalizations about patterns and relationships for the area as a whole and/or for particular distance zones and/or landscape types within it. Summarize these and relate to the theoretical concepts of the discipline.

It may be helpful to suggest two concluding problems which lead towards an appreciation of regional synthesis. Many of the components studied must be used in attempting to solve the problems and so their interaction must be weighed and considered.

Two problems of regional synthesis
1 In which village would you locate a new shop, where in the village would

55

you locate it and what type of goods would you sell? State clearly the guiding principles you have observed in making your choice.

2 Modify Keeble's urban growth simulation model[11] for choosing three villages to expand within the next decade.

References and sources for elaboration of methodology suggested

1 J. P. COLE and C. A. M. KING, *Quantitative Geography*, Wiley, 1968, ch. 3.

2 J. A. EVERSON and B. P. FITZGERALD, *Settlement Patterns*, Longman, 1969, ch. 9

3 TIDSWELL and BARKER, *Quantitative Methods: an Approach to Socio-Economic Geography*, U.T.P., 1971, ch. 5.

4 EVERSON and FITZGERALD, *op. cit.*, ch. 7.

5 TIDSWELL and BARKER, *op. cit.*, ch. 7.

6 *Ibid.*, ch. 5.

7 MITCHELL, *Historical Geography*, E.U.P., 1954, ch. 4.

8 TIDSWELL and BARKER, *op. cit.*, ch. 7.

9 EVERSON and FITZGERALD, *op. cit.*, ch. 7.

10 S. GREGORY, *Statistical Methods and the Geographer*, Longman, 1963.

11 D. KEEBLE, 'School Teaching and Urban Geography: Some New Approaches', *Geography*, Vol. 54 Part 1, January 1969.

P. J. AMBROSE, *Analytical Human Geography*, Longman, 1969.

The village summary

Date of survey..........................Student's name..............................

Name of village..Sample number............

Landscape type............................. Distance zone.............................

Expected town for retail trading ....

1 Estimated property values: 10 = high: 1 = low ....

2 Unique/not unique physical site ....

3 Shortest road distance to nearest town in miles .... in kms ....

4 Distance to nearest A road yards .... metres ....

5 Accessibility index (time/frequency) ....

6 Amenities for recreation ....

7 Population .... decline/growth/static   Significant date.........

8 Shape of village .... Shape of parish..........................

9 Complementary terrain   Yes/No

10 Commercial amenities: enter numbers and if appropriate type of shop
   Shops..
   Pub.............. Garage............... Primary school..............
   Secondary school............... P.O................ Police station.................
   Church and/or chapel..................

11 Optimum placing of commercial amenities   Yes/No

12 Number of houses built since 1960...

13 New building related to: physical terrain/road network/neither

14 Industry present/not present. See separate questionnaire for details.
15 From socio-economic summary sheets state:

    (a) % of people buying group 1 goods in village ....
    (b) % of people buying group 2 goods in expected retail town..............
    (c) % of people moving outside of area for 6b...................................

Group leaders transfer to area summary sheets.

Village survey area summary sheet

Study Area			Landscape Type				Distance Zone		
Villages	1	2	3	4	5	6	7	8	9	10
Features										
1										
2										
3a										
3b										
4a										
4b										
5										

Village survey questionnaire

Name of Village   *Number of House*

1 Where do you go to buy the following:

    (a) groceries   (b) milk
    (c) bread   (d) meat

2 Where do you shop for:

    (a) hardware   (b) shoes
    (c) men's clothes   (d) women's clothes
    (e) furniture   (f) electrical goods (TV)
    (g) hairdressing   (h) fuel

3 Where do you obtain the following services:

    (a) dentist   (b) doctor
    (c) optician   (d) chemist
    (e) hospital

4 Where do you obtain the following services:

    (a) lawyer   (b) accountant
    (c) auctioneer   (d) veterinary surgeon
    (e) banking

5 Where is your nearest:

    (a) post office   (b) policeman

6 Where do you go for the following entertainments:

    (a) cinema   (b) theatre

  (c) dancing   (d) bingo
  (e) public house   (f) sports fixture

7 Which place of worship do you attend?
8 Which secondary school do your children attend?
9 Do you own a car?   Can you obtain petrol in the village?
10 Where is your place of work?
   What type of work do you do?
11 What is your means of travel: car/bus/cycle/walk
12 From which town is your newspaper delivered?

XII A model hypothetical approach to urban fieldwork†

This unit, devised by Brian FitzGerald, is not set out in quite such detail as that described by Tidswell in section XI, but it represents a very similar approach.

FitzGerald identifies the nature of the central area in a town as the object of study, and then formulates four hypotheses concerned with this. The field work needed to test these involves not only observation (for determining land uses) but survey (for calculating pedestrian densities) and library work (for discovering rateable values). Thus not only is the scope of field work changed in relation to the selection of material, but techniques of work are supplemented, integrating other activities into the traditional methods of observation which has formed the keystone of much valuable school work in the past.

FitzGerald's cautionary note about the indiscriminate use of questionnaire techniques is a timely reminder, however, that some discrimination and concern needs to be exercised on behalf of those who are part of the survey canvass. One can well imagine that some inhabitants of well-known fieldworked areas must breathe heavy sighs every time an eager student approaches them, clipboard in hand. Opinion pollsters, market researchers, and local government survey teams may be unconscious conspirators in reducing the value of material gained in face-to-face contact, and in reducing the willingness of some members of the public to spare time answering questions. As FitzGerald points out, the material may well be already available in another place; in any case, survey work of this kind should be done with much preliminary preparation in order to prune out questions that are superfluous or irrelevant to the work being done. One of the problems with field work is often not that there is a lack of information, but that it has been collected with no clear idea of what end products may emerge. Merely to gather indiscriminate data from the environment is time-wasting and not particularly edifying; given a defined end purpose the nature of the information collected may itself be shaped.

The background to this kind of work is explored more fully by John Everson in chapter 4, Part 2, 'Fieldwork in school geography'.

†B. P. FitzGerald

Most British schools are either within or very close to urban areas where the sixth form may carry out a great range of urban field work. It is assumed that students who are involved in the type of approach outlined here will have carried out some urban work at various stages in their school careers. The introductory note on the background theory is kept as short as possible and includes only material that is relevant to the exercises that follow. It is firmly emphasized that work of this nature should be an integrated part of a study of urban geography ideally continuing on from work done in earlier years.

Two further points should be mentioned at this stage: the first is that field work is here defined to include work in all sources of data which may allow the development or testing of hypotheses and theories. Thus it is considered that work done in the rates office or on census returns in the public library is just as much an indispensable part of urban field work as is the plotting of urban land use on to a 50" base map.

The second point concerns the use of questionnaire surveys. These are indispensable to a comprehensive piece of field work, although it is felt that there is no need to cover all aspects of urban geography, especially if this (as seems likely in many cases) will lead to problems with the local authorities. There are many occasions when the direct questioning of the public may go against the wishes of the local planning authority. Where questionnaire surveys are being considered, these should always be done with their agreement, in case saturation occurs with the subsequent alienation of the public towards later professional approaches. In addition to this the local planning authority may have just the information required from an earlier survey, in an easily assimilated form, or indeed, it may wish to enlist the help of the school in question by asking them to collect data which would be beneficial to both the planning department and the school.

General background
Only one aspect of the urban system is examined here – that is the nature of the central area, and even here no attempt is made to be comprehensive. Urban functions are those which profit most from being located at points with a relatively high degree of accessibility to customers or suppliers located within the town's field of influence. Of course the most highly accessible location is that which is closest to the focus of routes, at the centre of what will develop into the town. The functions in the town located closest to this point are those that are most able to pay for such locations. Inevitably there is competition for the most accessible locations which results in the raising of the price of land to the level to which the highest bidders are willing to go. Fig. 21 shows graphically the rent paying ability of two firms (a) and (b).

Firm (a) is one that is able to capitalize more successfully from being at the centre in the most accessible location, while firm (b) is rather more indifferent about its location and can compete successfully only at a distance from the centre greater than o-p. Firms of type (a) are ones which react most strongly to variations in customers and to whom pedestrian traffic, representing potential custom, is of utmost importance. These firms are, of course, the leaders in generating such traffic in a town's central business district. A discussion of pedestrian traffic and its association with large stores is to be found in Everson and FitzGerald's *Inside the City*.[1] Firms of type (a) may be considered to be shops such as department stores, whose turnover would drop

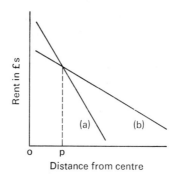

Fig 21. Bid-rent curves for two firms (a) and (b), competing for central locations

dramatically in any site other than one with the highest degree of accessibility. Firms at the other end of the scale are those less able to compete for the most accessible location, but because of their greater degree of indifference concerning location (their bid-rent curve has a lower gradient) they tend to find themselves at a relative advantage in the more outlying districts and are there able to compete more successfully.

The situation should give a simple zonation of land-use with shops of type (a) and (b) being located in the innermost zones, and firms and other land uses less able to compete being located in the outer zones. The degree of

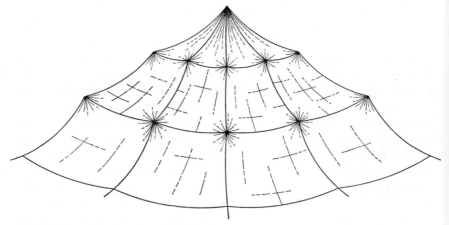

Fig 22. Generalized surface of land values within a city (after Berry)

accessibility and the rental values cannot be represented simply as a cone, with values peaking at its apex, as this denies the existence of a road system within the town. This, by its nature, produces ridges of a relatively high degree of accessibility culminating in local peaks at the crossing of major routes. Such a surface of accessibility is shown in fig. 22 the concept of accessibility here being directly related to the land values for the reasons stated above.

Hypotheses
Through previous work carried out both in the sixth form and at earlier stages in the school, the students will have been brought to this point and will have been led to develop a series of hypotheses which may be tested in the field. A selection of such hypotheses is listed below

1 that the most accessible locations will be indicated by the pattern and intensity of flow within the central business district
2 that because of more intense competition at the most accessible region of the town, land values will be at their highest there
3 that the areas of highest land value will correspond to areas of maximum pedestrian density (both declining with distance from the centre)
4 that a zonal pattern of land use within the centre will be discernible, indicating differential ability to compete for the most accessible locations.

Many other hypotheses based on this limited piece of theoretical work may be constructed, some being listed in D. P. Chapallaz *et al.* (1970)[2] and others being quite readily brought to mind with a little thought.

These hypotheses will have been based on previous experience of the students (personal observation in their own town, prior teaching and reading) and in all probability the teacher will have guided the students to make the hypotheses for themselves in class.

Data to prove the validity of such hypotheses will have to be collected by the students, and will form a central part of their practical work. Some methods of data collection for the four hypotheses noted above is given below:

1 A 'static pedestrian count' is undertaken to collect data that will illustrate the general pattern of pedestrian movement. Flows may be measured into, out of and within the CBD and the results will indicate those intersections and stretches of pavement exposed to the maximum pedestrian activity. The timing of counts should avoid those periods where non-shopping activity is significant (e.g. work rush-hours). The results of the count should be recorded on worksheets. The count should last a predetermined time (e.g. three minutes) and be taken from points near the centre of short stretches of pavement between road junctions. These 'count-sections' should normally be of the order of fifty to one hundred and fifty feet length (see fig. 23). Pedestrian movement in both directions should be noted separately. An alternative is for observers to note the movement of pedestrians into and out of road intersections thus giving more detail about direction of flow (see Chapallaz *et al.*).

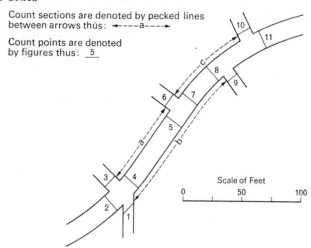

Fig 23. Sketch map showing suitable positions for count points and sections on a hypothetical road network

Location	Time	Moving into intersection*	Moving out of intersection*
Count point No. 1 2 etc			
	Totals		

Static pedestrian count recording sheet

* 'Moving to left', 'Moving to right' may be substituted here if the count is being taken from the centre of count sections.

Location	Length (ft)	Time	Number of pedestrians	Pedestrian density (per 100 ft)
Count section a b etc				
		Average		

These counts should be averaged rather than totalled

Moving pedestrian count recording sheet

NB Count points 1 to 11 are here given for precise information concerning the junctions. Slightly less detailed information using smaller numbers of observers may be obtained by taking counts from the centre of the count sections.

2 Land values as such are not readily available in Britain, except that it is possible to collect some data concerning particularly house prices from estate agents. However, this data would be far too sparse to give any real indication of land values in a shopping district. It is possible, however, to make use of rateable values, which are usually available for public inspection at the rates' office at the local town hall. Prior notice should, of course, be given to the chief rating officer. The rateable values are given for each building, street by street, and are, in effect, the local authority's view of the value of the land and buildings in terms of the rent likely to be realized each year. The values can be recorded directly on to the relevant 50″ plans. To make allowance for the various sizes of plots, the rateable value may later be reduced to a 'front-foot' basis, by dividing the gross rateable value for each building by the length of its frontage. Frontage rather than area is taken, not only for ease of computation, but also because it is the length of street frontage rather than area which weighs most heavily in assessment.

3 'Pedestrian density' is the number of pedestrians per unit length of pavement. It is normally convenient to take this unit as 100 feet. Count sections, which are the lengths of pavement over which the counts are taken, are generally between fifty and four hundred feet in length, so that the observed figure for the number of pedestrians has to be reduced or increased proportionately to allow the standard unit of one hundred feet. They should be continuous and have a similar character throughout, that is not be interrupted by vacant lots, car parks, or intersections with other streets (see fig. 23). The counts are taken by an observer walking at a steady pace through the count section. He should count the number of pedestrians he passes both in the opposite direction and those whom he overtakes. Window-shoppers may be included, but not people actually on shop premises. An example of a moving pedestrian count recording sheet is given on page 62.

4 Data for this hypothesis is collected by direct observation of the land use of each building, and then plotted on to a 50″ base map as a number code. A suggested classification of urban land use is given in Chapallaz et al.

After the collection of the data it is important that it is presented in some diagrammatic form prior to further discussion and analysis.

Pedestrian flows may be represented on a tracing overlay superimposed on a 25″ map of the CBD. This would show both peaking of flows and the various nodes or focii of pedestrian movement.

Rateable values per front foot should be plotted directly on to a 25″ base-map, each building then being shaded according to some suitable classification, varying, perhaps, from green through yellow to red for the highest front foot rateable values.

Pedestrian densities may be plotted as flow lines on an urban transect along the lines indicated in Chapallaz et al., p. 13. This form of representation also allows direct, but subjective, comparison to be made between various sets of data collected in the town (e.g. rateable values, land-use, pedestrian flow and height of buildings).

The land use of the central areas is best plotted directly from the 50″ field sheet on to a 25″ plan and then coloured according to the six or so broad categories given in fig. 25. This data would also be plotted on the urban transects.

Hypothesis testings

Hypotheses 1 and 2 may be testing objectively only with some difficulty, but hypothesis 3, dealing with land value and pedestrian density may be analysed more successfully. Neither is an independent variable, although there is probably some dependence of land value on pedestrian density because of customer generation. As is suggested on p. 59, however, they both should decline with distance from the centre; therefore some correlation analysis may be carried out. Fig. 24(a) shows the plot of land values (expressed as rateable values) as the dependent variable on the Y-axis, against the distance from centre as the independent variable on the X-axis, and (b) shows the plot of pedestrian density as the dependent variable on the Y-axis dependent upon the independent variable – again distance from the centre – on the X-axis.

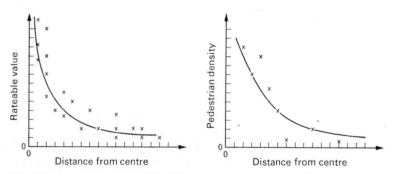

Fig 24. Graphs to show the relationship between distance from the centre of a town and (a) rateable value (b) pedestrian density

The precise relationship between variables such as these may be found through simple regression analysis, or more simply still through some form of rank correlation such as Spearman's. Reference to these methods may be made in any standard statistical text. These will give also the degree of significance that may be attached to the results.

Hypothesis 4, dealing with the zonation of land use is more difficult to test as a hypothesis, though it is possible to indicate whether there is any degree of zoning to the land use. One simple method is to place concentric circles, centred on the CBD with radii of (say) one tenth, two tenths, three tenths of a mile, and so on. In this way a number of annular zones are produced. The proportions of the various land uses may then be worked out for each zone, and the results tabulated as shown in fig. 25. A similar sort of analysis may be carried out in a much finer manner within the CBD to find if there is any regular zoning of shop types. Reference to this type of analysis may be found in Chapallaz *et al.*, Everson and FitzGerald,[3] and Haggett.[4]

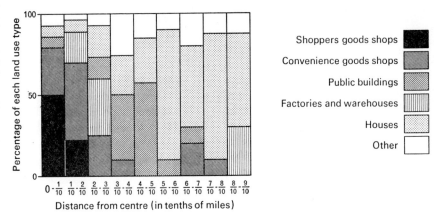

Fig 25. Diagram to show the relationship between proportions of urban land use and distance from the centre of a town

The presence of such a zoning may suggest that there is a differential ability between land-use types in competing for the most accessible locations, although other considerations will inevitably be drawn out in discussion.

The foregoing has dealt with only a minute proportion of the material which is available for this type of work on towns and cities. As suggested earlier (page 61) other hypotheses will easily suggest themselves with this material. But reference should be made to other topics and data which help, through this type of approach, to characterize the processes at work in urban areas. Carrol (in Norborg)[5] has carried out interesting work in Zurich on the price variation and range of type of certain goods throughout the city. Elsewhere, census material, particularly the 1966 'one in ten' census has a deal of data concerning population densities, socio-economic groupings and so on, by census enumeration districts. Some ways in which such material may be handled is given in Everson and FitzGerald.[1] Reference is also made to work concerning the delimitation of fields of influence within the city, again a section of study that leads to some understanding of the processes at work within a city.

References

1 J. A. EVERSON and B. P. FITZGERALD, *Inside the City*, Longman, 1972.

2 D. P. CHAPPALLAZ *et al.,* 'Hypothesis testing in field studies', *Teaching Geography No. 11*, Geographical Association, Sheffield, 1970.

3 J. A. EVERSON and B. P. FITZGERALD, *Settlement Patterns*, Longman, 1969, p. 26.

4 P. HAGGETT, *Locational Analysis in Human Geography*, Arnold, 1965, p. 158.

5 K. NORBORG, ed., *I.G.U. Symposium in Urban Geography*, Lund, 1962.

Part Two

New developments and their consequences

1 New developments in geography†

As we go through the 1970s it is evident to all geographers that a considerable methodological debate is proceeding in the discipline.[1]* Systematic geographers dispute with regionalists; quantifiers with non-quantifiers; exponents of model-building with defenders of more traditional approaches; those who believe in the development of generalizing and predictive models with those who feel that geography will always be concerned with retrospective explanations of the unique. In such situations, the temperature can sometimes be lowered by improving the flow of information between the sets of protagonists and by giving one group an improved insight into the thinking of the other. This, perhaps, is one of the prime aims of this book.

In the welter of disagreement about which specific methods should be used in geographical education we are, perhaps, overlooking a more fundamental question: what do we conceive to be the aims of geographical education? What special skills and knowledge should a geographical training bestow? A high level of factual knowledge about large areas of the earth's surface and how their inhabitants live (which we might call 'coverage')? An ability to characterize a region or country and to capture in print its essential nature ('regional characterization')? A highly developed sense of the two-way interplay of man and his physical environment ('ecology')? Or a specialist understanding of the role that location and distance play in the operation of the social, economic and political processes that bring about patterns of man-made phenomena and changes in those patterns ('spatial analysis')? The world expects trained geographers to be expert at the first three activities and it has not been disappointed one hopes. But now the fourth aim has been accepted, in some quarters, as paramount.[2] Emphasis on this aim does not exclude consideration of the others (especially the third), since the aims are not mutually exclusive.[3] It does, however, imply a move in emphasis from regional (form-orientated) to systematic (process-orientated) work; from subjective-qualitative to objective-quantitative handling of information; from unique to generalized explanations; and, often, from retrospective to predictive modes of study. The discussion is not really about which of these various methods of working are best, since methods can be judged only in terms of what they are trying to achieve. Thus clearly it is pointless to teach a regional course if we are trying to develop space analytical expertise and

* Figures in square brackets indicate references at end of unit.

†Peter Ambrose

futile to teach urban growth models if we are intent on achieving coverage.[4] The discussion is surely about aims not methods, about ends not means. This can hardly be emphasized too strongly. To accept recently developed thinking about aims is to accept most, if not all, of the work in this book. Similarly the work cannot reasonably be rejected unless the aims are thought to be mistaken.

Before I attempt to delineate the essential differences between the various modes of work in geography, I should perhaps declare my interests. Because I work in a university it might be assumed that my whole interest is to plead for the adoption of a new approach to school work in order to ease the transition between school and university. This would in fact be a legitimate plea. Experience in dealing with a wide variety of student problems at Sussex has convinced me that any development that reduces the difficulty of the transition is to be warmly welcomed. But equally I am aware that only a small minority of those who specialize in geography at school will be going on to read the subject at university. And for people who leave school at fifteen or sixteen there will have been no specialization anyway. Yet I feel that a new approach to the discipline is needed for these groups as much as for any other.

I would argue that recent developments in thinking, and recent experimentation in the classroom, should be seen not simply as constituting better preparation for 'academic' geographers but simply as better preparation for life. This is a large and disputable claim for which there is no evidence either way. Like most educational generalizations, it is really a statement of faith, or, to be a little more brutal, of prejudice. It is based on a personal view that any line of approach that stresses judgment and decision-making by the individual, that poses questions of value, that enables a model of a real-life situation to develop in the classroom and that recognizes societal problems as the proper objects of intellectual endeavour, cannot be too wide of the mark. It also stems from the view that education, at any level, should try to get people to ask the right sort of questions in the right sort of order, rather than hope to give them 'right' answers. But clearly this depends upon one's view about the existence of any 'right' answers.

There is one other important preliminary point to be made. It may be widely believed that the split between traditionalists and innovators is a grouping along school-versus-university lines. Clearly this book is one piece of evidence against such a belief. Another, less salutary, piece of evidence is the existence in nearly all university departments of deep divisions of opinion about these issues – divisions that it would be pointless to deny. All too often the forces of reaction are mustered to frustrate changes in course structure. This is to some extent as it should be – bandwagons are notoriously unreliable vehicles – but there could be a real problem in the near future. Bright sixth-formers, already introduced to new and demanding concepts by progressive teachers, could well find themselves in first year university or training college courses that are little more than extensions of the present majority of A-level courses. This would be one more reason for protest – and a perfectly legitimate one. It would be as well, therefore, to bear in mind that this contribution, although the only one from a university geographer, should not be seen as some Olympian attempt to spread the gospel from on high (if such a confusion of theology is acceptable!). Rather, it should be seen as a contribution from a co-innovator working in another part of the educational system.

The essential characteristics of recent trends

It is a vast and difficult task to sum up what has happened recently in the discipline. My interpretation will no doubt be challenged at every point by someone or other. But then so, I suspect, would anybody else's interpretation. We are all well enough aware of traditional modes of study, and I will not dwell upon them. They tend to emphasize factual learning and empiricism as opposed to theory formation, study by region rather than by topic, and a concern with the current distributions rather than the processes by which they evolve. This is, of course, a simplification, but one must start somewhere, preferably with a clear thesis. My main thesis will be that the changes can be summed up as a move from a factual orientation to an orientation concerned with concepts, methods and values.[5] I shall deal with each of these in turn, aware, however, that they are not mutually exclusive.

Concepts

One general concept[6] underlying a great deal of recent work is the idea that, essentially, we are seeking to understand societal processes that, because they give rise to repeating arrangements in space, are themselves likely to be repeating and thus predictable. Distributions (of settlement, crops, urban blight, nuclear power stations, stock-broker belts, or almost anything else in the landscape) are clearly not random.[7] Therefore, we believe, the decision processes that bring them about are not random either. Therefore there are regularities in human behaviour, both in space and time, to be discerned, mapped, explained and predicted. We are thus seeking to see how things work, not to spend a great deal of time describing what they look like. Our interest is very much in process as well as form. This may seem too trite to be said. But how many field weeks, for example, end up with a mass of emphemeral data about specific forms (such as crop patterns or village spacing) rather than with some clear conclusions about the processes which have produced the forms?

Much recent work, too, has tended to concern itself, implicitly rather than explicitly, with the discernment of locational principles. Of course we have not been entirely without principles before. But they tended to lack general validity. The principle that volcanic plugs are defensible, and that this explains the location of Edinburgh, is plausible enough – until one asks why certain volcanic plugs do not have Edinburgh or, indeed, any city upon them. The same general criticism applies to gaps and gap towns. And river terraces and

71

settlement. Many of these principles are, to use planning terminology, indicative but not prescriptive. They are necessary but not sufficient conditions to explain the phenomena concerned.

It could be argued that the number of thoroughly reliable, and useful geographical principles does not exceed two (although one is always open to higher bids). They are:

(a) *The distance principle:* that the distance, however measured, between two locations conditions the degree of interaction between them.

(b) *The spatial implication principle:* that once an event has occurred at a location, the probability of other events occurring in the vicinity is either increased or diminished.

At first glance the first principle might seem totally obvious and the second totally incomprehensible. I will therefore try to set out the specific operational concepts which I believe have been based on these principles.

The *distance principle* underlines the various formulations of the gravity model. This combines, in varying degrees of sophistication, the two common-sense propositions that the propensity of people, goods or information to move from a location to a destination is directly dependent upon the 'pull' of the destination and inversely dependent on the 'distance'. The trick, of course, is to measure pull and distance in such a way that the resultant predictions are reasonably accurate. Since such important issues as the success of a proposed shopping centre, the degree of use of a new road link, or the likely demand in a given area for school places in five years' time depend to some extent on predicting the movement of people (as they migrate, shop, go to work, etc.) the gravity model is clearly an important concept if it can produce reliable predictions of these phenomena.

The interaction between two locations in terms of such things as social contact, information and disease is also generally regarded to be inversely related to the distance between them. This has been well demonstrated for social contact in terms of 'marriage distances' and the closely related question of the spatial distribution of friends and acquaintances.[10] The reliability of the negative relationship between information flow and distance has been heavily undermined by the mass media and the consequent partial conquest of distance, but some types of information (for example, concerning new farming practices) still tend to be accepted, if not received, in a gradual manner that overcomes distance relatively slowly.[11] There are clear similarities here between the spread of information of the 'seeing is believing' type (for example, new fashions in clothes) and the spread of such diseases as influenza or foot and mouth. Conceptually, either could be well simulated by a stochastic diffusion model (see below).

The *spatial implication principle* is likewise of fundamental importance and wide generality. It is, perhaps, basic to much recent thinking because of the obvious stress it lays on dynamic and cumulative processes. It also underlies the whole tradition of systems thinking. The principle applies to almost anything in the lanscape. For example the location of an airport, motorway link or tunnel has implications for land uses in the vicinity; the location of a highrise block of offices has implications (not always well perceived) for local transport planning; the location of a supermarket in a new shopping centre decreases the probability of another supermarket arriving; the closure of a factory will affect activity, and thus land use, in the vicinity. It might be argued that the tracing out of these implications, the understanding of the mechanisms by which they have effect and the prediction of the land-use changes that might result are the central aims of geographical analysis. Such analysis is distinctively geographical because space and distance are treated so overtly. In all the cases mentioned, the effect of the change falls off with increasing distance from the point of change (in time as well as in space). The study may well appear economic or sociological in terms of the discipline or disciplines from which much of the theory or operational techniques are drawn. But because developments of this sort occur at specific places, and have effects on specific fields, the geographer or locational analyst also has his particular skills and models to contribute.[12]

Recent attempts to encompass the essential and many-faceted relationships between events at one place and the resultant or concomitant events at another have tended to fall into a systems framework and to use the rather sophisticated terminology of general systems theory. Thus we have the 'activity systems' of Chapin[13], the 'urban systems' of Warneryd[14] and the 'systems planning' of McLoughlin.[15] There is no doubt that many of these concepts are useful in focusing attention on the mechanisms by which one activity affects another, or by which activities express themselves in land uses. It might be held however, that this usefulness is sometimes diminished by a certain tendency on the part of systems devotees not only to state the obvious (which is often forgivable), but to state it in an incomprehensible fashion (which is not).

On a smaller or individual scale of study there has been a strong move recently towards a more behavioural approach to human action in relation to space, coupled with a strong suspicion that analyses based on the concept of some omniscient, omnipotent, 'economic' man may be fundamentally unsound. Man, it is argued, works and makes decisions in an environment which he perceives in an imperfect and indeed fragmentary fashion. His range of choice is thus less than that likely to be attributed to him by some trained external observer. His motivations, likewise, may be other than purely and predictably economic. He may value leisure, 'psychic income' or an overt display of his status more than he values strict economic returns. This is inconvenient but must be allowed for.

On the particular issues of the extent to which man acts from purely economic motives, a study carried out by Wolpert is of great importance.[16] He devised what appeared to be the economically optimum pattern of farm

73

production in middle Sweden and compared the actual pattern with this optimum. His conclusions concerning the differences in knowledge, environmental understanding and goals exhibited by the farmers, and the socio-economic variables by which these differences appeared to be conditioned, led him to introduce into geographical literature the 'satisficer' and 'optimizer' concepts. 'Optimizers' appear to correspond to 'economic' man. 'Satisficers', one suspects, are what most of us really are – individuals anxious to succeed in a material sense but not to the exclusion of all other considerations.

This study has been fairly influential in instigating further research along behavioural lines, some of it tending to state self-evident truths in weighty jargon. The field has been usefully summarized by a recent book by Cox and Golledge, two leading exponents.[17] Since the emphasis is so heavily on individual decision-making processes, and the measurement of such things as preferences, values and rates of learning, various concepts and techniques have been borrowed from social psychology.[18]

One interesting area of behavioural research has been the attempts to analyse 'subjective distance'[19] and 'mental maps'.[20] It seems evident that the individual's perception of the distance to a point is heavily biased by a number of factors including the desirability of reaching the point, the completeness of information about the point and the perceived social nature of the point. Our mental map is a vision of reality glimpsed through cultural, social and individual filters. It may bear very little relation to objective reality (whatever that may be). Yet it is the map upon which we act; any understanding or prediction of our actions depends upon some understanding of our mental map.[21]

Other research has concentrated on our perception of the physical environment. Lynch's pioneer work[22] on perceptions of various North American urban environments has been followed by a range of perceptual studies dealing with such environments as the Great Plains[23] and the Arctic.[24] So far progress in this important field seems none too impressive, partly because few geographers are sufficiently well-read in the literature of psychology. But it seems likely that this is an area of research that will continue to expand because of its obvious and vital relevance to the understanding of man's activities, choices and movements in space.

One other important conceptual development that should at least be mentioned is the recent re-thinking that has taken place about the effective meaning of 'environment' for the geographer. It has for some time been evident that most of us live our lives in an urban environment and that, if we take the traditional view that geography is somehow concerned with man/land relationships, then 'land' is effectively the city. Robson has recently given precision to this idea when he stresses:

... the importance of the effects of milieu on urban social structure. Within the term 'milieu' is included not only the physical environment of housing conditions but also the less tangible factors of room density and area density, of the whole complex of such psychological factors as attitudes and of spatial location relative to facilities within the town and other people or types of people within a given local area.[25]

This concept of milieu is clearly significant if we want to understand why people behave as they do in a given area and what makes surroundings bearable or alienating to live in.

Methods
The first and most fundamental point to be made here is that recent work seems to have been reaching out towards more validly scientific procedures. Geographers have always been closely concerned with observation, but they have not always had good answers to the question 'observation for what?' This is not an appropriate place for a full discussion of scientific methods.[26] But we might note that observation is but one aspect of the sequence that, ideally, includes the stages of problem definition, hypothesis formation, hypothesis testing (by observation and analysis of data), refinement and modification of hypothesis, and further observation. Translated into practical terms, this means that full discussion concerning the hypotheses to be tested, the variables to be measured and the measurement techniques to be used must be carried out before the field survey work is begun. Field work, or any other investigation, should never be embarked upon unless everyone involved is clear about the specific aims of the exercise and the sort of answers that might be expected to emerge.[27] Equally, the methods by which the data is to be analysed must be thought out in advance because they might well condition the form in which the data should be collected. This may all sound utterly elementary. Yet, in my experience, more undergraduate and graduate research projects are ruined by overlooking these basic points of research methodology than by any other cause.

In terms of specific methods, we have seen in recent years a long overdue improvement in the degree of precision with which information is handled and hypotheses are tested in geography. There is no reason why any scientific discipline, physical or social, should not use the techniques developed by statisticians or by specialists in other disciplines, if the use of such techniques adds to our understanding of the relationships which interest us.[28] While, arguably, a decent analysis of Hamlet can perhaps be done without a computer, the analysis of a population census cannot. The problem in geography is not so much whether to use quantitative techniques but rather, given a particular problem, which technique or programme to use.

There has recently been a widespread increase in the use of the standard statistical techniques of *correlation and regression*, since many geographical problems involve the degree to which two variables correlate.[29] *Multivariate* techniques (multiple regression, factor analysis and principle components analysis) have also been widely used recently, especially in arriving at

75

valid regionalizations and groupings. These areal grouping exercises can be carried out at all scales, from national level[30] down to the delineation of small social areas within a city.[31] They represent a solid advance on the sort of thinking that still asserts, 'We don't make the regions we study. They're already there.' Valid groupings of space into regions are, of course, not already there. We have to make our areal units of study in the light of such criteria as the purpose of the research, the choice of appropriate differentiating variables, the scale at which the data (e.g. census data) is available and the resources available for research.

Other quantitative techniques have been applied to the measurement of distributions. Patterns of points, lines and areas have all been analysed in terms of *nearest neighbour* techniques.[32] The patterning of areas in particular has been studied by means of the *continuity ratio*.[33] It would seem that these techniques, like correlation/regression, are ideally suited to geographical study since the starting point of our analyses, indeed the central problem of many studies, is some examination of distribution. The comparison of two or more distributions, separated in space or in time or in both, is frequently a key aspect of the work, and such comparisons can often be carried out by nearest neighbour, contiguity, or the closely related quadrat count techniques.[34]

Network analysis has also been vigorously developed recently and has been useful not only in giving precision to the measurement of social, communication and transport networks, but also in forging a link between physical and human studies.[35] This set of ideas (like nearest neighbour ideas) was in fact first developed in relation to the measurement of physical phenomena (notably river systems) and has been imported into human work most obviously by the 'two cultures' men of Cambridge and Bristol. Network analysis seems to have fairly obvious practical applications and has been used in various road planning situations,[36] in at least one historical study,[37] and as a regionalization technique.[38] There also seem to be promising possibilities for adapting the technique to the measurement of social networks.[39]

Another technique that has been widely used recently is *trend surface mapping*.[40] With this technique (borrowed from geophysics and other natural sciences) human phenomena normally gathered as values at points in space, and thus producing a 'spot-height' distribution, can be smoothed or generalized into a surface which can be expressed in the form of a set of equations. The aim of this exercise is ' . . . to disentangle the smooth, broader, regional patterns of variation from the non-systematic, local and chance variations.' It is often possible to discern residuals or local anomalies from the surface thus measured and to see whether any systematic explanation of these residuals can be found. Thus, as with many other techniques of this sort, the aim is not simply to state a situation more precisely but also to uncover anomalies that would not otherwise be discerned and to develop hypotheses which themselves give rise to further research.

Mention, perhaps, should be made of *markov chain* formulations which deal with the movement of any defined phenomena from a starting state through a set of subsequent states in accordance with a matrix of transition probabilities (often established by reference to empirical data).[41] The probability of any element in the starting matrix moving from S_i to S_j is expressed as P_{ij}, and this probability is stable over time. One easily understood study deals with the movement of areas in various American cities up (or down) the rental hierarchy over a period of time.[42] This technique, like several to be discussed shortly, has the feature of stressing evolution through time and is thus well in line with the recent emphases on process.

Another recent development which is orientated at least as much towards process as towards form, or which sees form as a clear expression of process, is the trend towards the use of *simulation* techniques. These are essentially models of developing situations which conform to certain rules abstracted and simplified from reality. It is possible to simulate a wide range of situations and, by speeding up the time scale, to observe their evolution in a short space of time. The great danger here is that in the formulation of the rules, in the speeding up of time or in some other way the simulation becomes a distortion, rather than an approximation, of reality.[43] But even so there is some educational benefit to be derived from discussing the ways in which the simulation does appear to mislead, and thus focusing on the real nature of the process being simulated. This could lead to the formulation by the group of a more realistic set of rules for the simulation.

One way in which simulation has been used is in the development of *operational games*, both in teaching and problem-solving situations. In view of the growing literature on this topic I would not presume to detail the educational benefits to be derived from role playing and spatial decision-making in a competitive situation. It might be as well to point out, however, that this is one area in which a method is diffusing up the educational hierarchy in that university courses (at Bristol and Sussex and perhaps elsewhere) now include an element of gaming, using games developed for younger learners. Movement in this direction is to be warmly welcomed. Operational gaming has, of course, been widely used in business training, conflict research and planning, and it is a technique that could be used in any situation where decisions have to be taken in a climate of uncertainty and competition. If nothing else, it appears to generate a high degree of involvement among participants of all ages and ability levels, and anything that does that is to be nurtured carefully.

Other, non-conflict, situations are well suited to simulation. For example, the diffusion of certain innovations,[44] of a Negro ghetto[45] and of a pattern of settlements[46] have all been attempted. The degree of correspondence between simulated and actual patterns is always difficult to evaluate simply because it is impossible to know how a given situation might have developed had it not developed as it did. This is the essential difference between most experimentation in the social sciences and laboratory experimentation in the physical sciences. In one case the experiments can be repeated and in the other they cannot. Morrill puts the aim of the social simulator neatly when he says of his ghetto simulation that, 'This similarity, rather than conformance, indicated that both the actual and the simulated patterns *could have occurred* according to the operation of the model. This is the crucial test of theory.' In other words, reality is but one of an infinite number of ways in which the situation might have developed and Morrill, if his simulation rules are good, is producing one of these ways with each repetition of his computer run. Sooner or later it should produce a pattern that corresponds exactly with reality.

Most simulation techniques, and certainly all games, make some allowance for the operation of what we call chance. Whether chance represents a truly random quality or whether it is our shorthand for the rational operation of factors which we do not understand is a philosophical issue beyond my competence. In many geographical models the chance element is accommodated by incorporating at some point, the drawing of random numbers (each possible outcome having been assigned a probability based on empirical evidence and/or common sense). Wherever this device is used the model becomes a *stochastic* or *Monte Carlo* model.[47] This appears so far to be the only way that we can allow for those apparently random events that condition and change so many social situations.

This hasty review of recently developed methods could perhaps end with some mention of *game theory*, which differs from gaming simulations in that it is a well-developed branch of mathematics. A paper by Peter Gould[48] provides the best introduction to this technique, which is essentially a device for arriving at an optimum set of strategies where two or more parties are in a conflict situation and certain information is known about the immediate outcome of particular choices. Gould's paper is an attempt to arrive at an optimum crop pattern for a region of Ghana, given that man's opponent, the weather, will act to minimize his returns. It would seem that this technique could be used to great advantage in a range of similar crop-choice situations, but so far there seems to have been little further development.

There is one general point about all these newly-developed or borrowed techniques. They are not, in themselves, geography. In the same way plumblines, slide-rules and scale models of buildings are not, in themselves, architecture. They are simply tools. The real aim of the geographical analyst, in my view, is to reach a better understanding of how man is organizing himself in space and, in some cases, to help produce more rational, efficient and socially desirable land-use patterns by participation in the planning profession. The aims are not really very different from those of the architect, except that the architect deals largely with internal rather than external space. Geography and architecture are about the physical manifestations in landscape of social, economic and political processes and values. The problem of understanding the relationships between form and function (with the additional complication that the latter generally changes faster than the former) are common to both disciplines. The tools of the trade are essential elements in reaching this understanding, but they should not condition the direction of advance or the ultimate aims of the activity either in architecture or geography.

Values

The discussion in the last paragraph leads naturally to a consideration of the role of values in geographical education. What, for example, are 'socially desirable land-use patterns'? It depends on one's social values. For too long, it seems, we have studied land-use patterns and changes without fully realizing that these are the physical embodiment of social, economic and political assumptions and judgments. Clearly there will be different opinions about the extent to which discussion about societal and individual values should find a place in our teaching, but surely it should be present somewhere (as it no doubt already is in many cases). To deny discussion of this sort might be interpreted by our students, perhaps correctly, as a confession of insecurity or even guilt about the values we hold concerning the nature of society.

The discussion is relevant here because more and more geographers are becoming involved in the planning profession where, day by day, and often perhaps subconsciously, decisions are made which reflect social values. Many examples could be given about the way in which social assumptions are translated into physical fabric. The arrangement of housing densities, the range of these density values, the placing of private and municipal estates, the zonation of industry and other planning decisions of this sort will condition the amount of social mixing that occurs in a new town (if we accept geographical principle number one: that proximity increases the likelihood of mixing).[49] We can create vast one-class areas at will. In fact Victorian and inter-war suburbs are full of such areas. We can allow the formation of areas of highly-clustered immigrant population or we could, conceivably, diffuse newcomers throughout the city. Which would be right? And who is to say? It is too important an issue to be left to the judgment of professional planners, however well-intentioned.[50] We should all be familiar with the issues and mechanisms involved, and discussion could surely start in schools.

Another clearly geographical issue involving value judgments is the controversy, now almost moribund, about the extent to which urban housing densities should be increased to save agricultural land.[51] Economically, this policy makes no sense at all; it would be far cheaper to bring in new agricultural land by other methods. But a little below the surface lies a political issue between rural and urban interests, an issue that should perhaps be discussed in more honest terms.

Similarly the whole issue of the conservation of rural landscape and amenity is inextricably bound up with interests and values. No doubt everybody agrees about the need to preserve beautiful countryside, to control the pollution of air and rivers, to maintain the green belts for the pleasure of urban dwellers. But what if an electricity board needs to transmit electricity across a valley, an industry discovers a cheaper process that will inevitably increase pollution or a factory in a green belt needs to expand to help the export drive? Who should decide how these conflicts between long term amenity and short term efficiency are to be resolved? And by reference to what scale of values?[52]

Our values are again inevitably involved when we begin to analyse imbalances in regional growth. Many recent studies, presumably reflecting some social conscience on the part of the authors, have concentrated on identifying areas of economic stress.[53] Action towards areas of this sort often resolves, essentially, into a choice between two alternatives; subsidy in a form which will renew activity, or a policy of encouraging out-migration, either by incentive or by simply doing nothing.[54] The fundamental question of values here is whether the rest of the economy should run the cost of subsidizing an area on the social grounds that people have a right to a fair share of prosperity without having to move out, and that community and family ties should not lightly be dislocated.[55]

One final issue might be identified. What should be the individual landowner's rights in respect of his land? Should he have complete control over development and use? Should he have a measure of control but be subject to external influence in the form of planning legislation? Or should government, acting on behalf of the whole community, own all the land? The questions are clearly fundamental to the way that, for example, a city centre evolves. In Britain, in a typical compromise, we adopt the second position. Other political systems adopt positions to the left or right. It is obviously a political issue but one which, even if it is not discussed, must be seen as a strong determinant on land-use patterns and evolution. But why should it not be discussed? Many sixth-formers are now entitled to vote. They are thus assumed to be politically mature. Yet perhaps we have tended to deal with questions of land use without a sufficiently honest and thorough examination of the motives and values of key decision-makers and in the belief that the issues are ethically and morally neutral. It is difficult to be neutral about urban blight, ghettos, or enormous speculative gains, nor should we attempt to be.[56]

Possible implications for school work

It is not really for me to indicate precisely how the school geography curriculum should be changed. This will be a matter for lengthy collective discussion. But from the review I have attempted I would abstract five possible implications for the future direction of school work:

1 A move *from a factually-based to a concept-based mode of study*. This is not to say that current work is without concepts or that future work should be without facts. It is all a matter of emphasis.

2 A move *from regional to systematic work*. If we are trying to study some process such as urban growth, social differentiation or shopping behaviour, we have to draw examples from a wide range of areas. It is no good looking

at one or two studies then waiting a year for the next region to come round before studying a few more. This move would seem to stem logically and inevitably from any increased emphasis on process rather than form.

3 A move *from compartmentalized to interdisciplinary* work. Most of the concepts and methods discussed have been developed in other disciplines. The values clearly are not exclusively geographical. The problems we examine are essentially interdisciplinary. So too, within the constraints of the time-table and the syllabus, should be our modes of study.

4 A move *from qualitative to quantitative statements.* Little need be said to justify this suggestion. There are obvious dangers that the techniques may condition the research, and obvious difficulties for all of us in learning new skills. But other related disciplines came to terms with these problems decades ago.

5 A move *from a lesser to a greater emphasis on values.* No one, least of all university lecturers, wish to have teachers indoctrinating people or stirring them up to right all the wrongs of society. But such fears seem to under-estimate both the teachers and the judgment of sixteen- to eighteen-year-olds. The suggestion is simply that it should be fully accepted that land-use patterns are physical expressions of the way a society organizes itself and that study of the form might well include more overt discussion of the organization.

References

1 See I. BURTON, 'The quantitative revolution and theoretical geography', *Canadian Geographer*, 1963, pp. 151–62, for a useful discussion of the issues involved. (This paper, together with another seven of the references that follow, is included in P. J. AMBROSE, *Analytical Human Geography*, Longman, 1969.)

2 See E. A. WRIGLEY, 'Changes in the philosophy of geography', ch. 1 in R. J. CHORLEY and P. HAGGETT, *Frontiers in Geographical Teaching*, Methuen 1965, for a historical review of changing modes of work in geography

3 For a brief discussion of geographical objectives, see D. HARVEY, *Explanation in Geography*, Arnold, 1969, ch. 1.

4 Reference to any of the classic, if compendious, regional textbooks should make this clear. It would be invidious to mention examples.

5 My thinking has no doubt been influenced here by one of the third-year courses taken by all members of the School of Social Sciences at Sussex – Concepts, Methods and Values in the Social Sciences.

6 It might be argued that the concepts isolated in this section, and others like them, may be the tropisms referred to by J. S. BRUNER, *The Process of Education*, Vintage Books (1963), pp. 6–7, and may, collectively, constitute the structure of the discipline of human geography.

7 Although various recent papers by L. CURRY and M. F. DACEY have been built on the thesis that although the processes that bring about specific

distributions are not random, they are, in fact, so complex that they can often best be replicated by using models incorporating principles of randomness.

8 For useful summaries of the models based upon gravitational ideas see G. A. P. CARROTHERS, 'An historical review of the gravity and potential concepts of human interaction', *Journal of the American Institute of Planners*, 1956, pp. 94–102 and G. OLSSON, '*Distance and Human Interaction*', Regional Science Research Institute, Philadelphia, 1965.

9 See R. L. MORRILL and F. R. PITTS, 'Marriage, migration and the mean information field; a study in uniqueness and generality', *Annals Association of American Geographers*, 1967, pp. 401 *et seq.*

10 See M. M. WEBBER, 'Culture, territoriality and the elastic mile', *Papers and Proceedings, Regional Science Association*, 1964, pp. 59–69.

11 For a useful annotated bibliography of spatial diffusion processes, see L. A. BROWN, *Diffusion Processes and Location*, Regional Science Research Institute, Philadelphia, 1968.

12 D. HARVEY, *Explanation in Geography*, Arnold, 1969, ch. 23, provides a useful introduction to this set of ideas.

13 F. S. CHAPIN, *Urban Land Use Planning*, Illinois, 1965, ch. 6.

14 O. WARNERYD *Interdependence in Urban Systems*, 1968.

15 J. B. MCLOUGHLIN, *Urban and Regional Planning*, 1969.

16 J. WOLPERT, 'The decision process in spatial context', *Annals Association of American Geographers*, 1964, pp. 537–558.

17 K. R. COX and R. G. GOLLEDGE, *Behavioural Problems in Geography: a Symposium*, Northwestern University, 1969.

18 As a perusal of the reading lists following several of the papers in the Cox and Golledge volume will show.

19 D. L. THOMPSON, 'New concept: subjective distance', *Journal of Retailing*, Spring 1963, pp. 1–6.

20 P. R. GOULD and R. R. WHITE, 'The mental maps of British school leavers', *Regional Studies*, 1968, pp. 161–182.

21 See D. HARVEY, *Explanation in Geography*, Arnold, 1969, ch. 14, for a useful review of the growth of these ideas, including some discussion of the valuable work of Bunge and Tobler

22 K. LYNCH, *The Image of the City*, M.I.T. Press, 1960.

23 T. F. SAARINEN, *Perception of the Drought Hazard on the Great Plains*, University of Chicago, 1966.

24 See the short paper by J. SONNENFELD, in D. LOWENTHAL, *Environmental Perception and Behaviour*, University of Chicago, 1967.

25 B. T. ROBSON, *Urban Analysis*, Cambridge, 1969, p. 244.

26 See Part II of D. HARVEY, *Explanation in Geography,* Arnold, 1969, for a full discussion of scientific method, especially as it applies to geography.

27 See pp. 10–12 of the author's book, *Analytical Human Geography*, Longman, 1969.

28 See M. J. MORONEY, *Facts from Figures*, Penguin, 1956, for a clear and full introduction to various useful standard techniques and L. J. KING, *Statistical Analysis in Geography*, Prentice-Hall, 1969, for some rather more advanced and specialist treatment.

29 See chs. 11 and 12 of S. GREGORY, *Statistical Methods and the Geographer*, Longman, 1963.

30 See C. A. MOSER and W. SCOTT, *British Towns*, Oliver and Boyd, 1961.

31 See ch. 4 of B. T. ROBSON, *Urban Analysis*, Cambridge, 1969.

32 See L. J. KING, 'A quantitative expression of the pattern of urban settlements in selected areas of the United States', *Tijdschrift voor Economische en Sociale Geografie*, 1962, pp. 1–7.

33 See the two final contributions, by R. C. GEARY and M. F. DACEY, in B. J. L. BERRY and D. F. MARBLE, *Spatial Analysis*, Prentice-Hall, 1968.

34 See A. GETIS, 'Temporal land use pattern analysis with the use of nearest neighbour and quadrat methods', *Annals Association of American Geographers*, 1964, pp. 391–399.

35 The fullest review of these techniques it to be found in P. HAGGETT'S chapter in R. J. CHORLEY and P. HAGGETT, *Models in Geography*, Methuen, 1967 (later also issued in three parts in paper-back editions from the same publishers), and in the subsequent book by the same authors, *Network Analysis in Geography*, Arnold, 1969.

36 W. L. GARRISON, 'Connectivity of the interstate highway system', *Papers and Proceedings, Regional Science Association*, 1960, pp. 121–137.

37 F. R. PITTS, 'A graph theoretic approach to historical geography', *Professional Geographer*, 1965/5, pp. 15–20.

38 J. D. NYSTUEN and M. F. DACEY, 'A graph theory interpretation of nodal regions', *Papers and Proceedings, Regional Science Association*, 1961, pp. 29–42.

39 A short unpublished paper on this topic is available from this author.

40 See R. J. CHORLEY and P. HAGGETT, 'Trend surface mapping in geographical research' *Transactions and Papers of the Institute of British Geographers*, No. 37, 1965, pp. 47–67.

41 See pp. 577–582 of D. HARVEY'S chapter in R. J. CHORLEY and P. HAGGETT, *Models in Geography*, Methuen, 1967.

42 W. A. V. CLARK, 'Markov chain analysis in geography: an application to the movement of rental housing areas', *Annals Association of American Geographers,* 1965, pp. 351–359.

43 See R. J. CHORLEY, 'Geography and analogue theory', *Annals Association of American Geographers*, 1964, pp. 127–137, for a useful discussion of these dangers and for a typology of models.

44 T. HAGERSTRAND, 'A Monte Carlo approach to diffusion', *European Journal of Sociology*, 1965, pp. 43–67.

45 R. L. MORRILL, 'The Negro ghetto, problems and alternatives', *Geographical Review*, 1965, pp. 339–361.

46 R. L. MORRILL, 'The development of spatial distribution of towns in Sweden: an historical predictive approach', *Annals Association of American Geographers,* 1963, pp. 1–14.

47 As are the simulation models specified above.

48 P. R. GOULD, 'Man against his environment: a game theoretic framework', *Annals Association of American Geographers,* 1963, pp. 290–297.

49 It might be an instructive exercise to choose a wide variety of towns, historic market towns, nineteenth-century industrial towns, recently expanded towns, 'Mark I' new towns, subsequent new towns, and so on, and to measure the following characteristics:

   i   the average population density

   ii the extent to which the densities of definable sub-areas vary from the mean (calculating perhaps the standard deviation)

   iii the extent to which high and low density areas intermingle.

Obviously population density does not exactly reflect the social status of an area, but it is quite a useful index. For a useful discussion about social structure and the spatial structure of towns, see ch. 3 of R. E. PAHL, *Patterns of Urban Life,* Longman, 1970.

50 For an extremely relevant contribution on this issue, and one that usefully illustrates applications of regression analysis and markov techniques, see B. J. L. BERRY, 'Monitoring trends, forecasting change, and evaluating goal-achievement in the urban environment: the ghetto expansion versus desegregation issue in Chicago as a case study', paper given at the Colston Research Symposium on Regional Forecasting, Bristol, 1970.

51 There is a vast literature on this topic, See, for example, P. SELF, *Cities in Flood,* Faber, 1961; G. WIBBERLEY, *Agriculture and Urban Growth,* Michael Joseph, 1959; R. H. BEST, 'Extent of urban growth and agricultural displacement in post-war Britain', *Urban Studies* 5 (1), 1968, pp. 1–23 and papers by the same author in *New Society,* 24 November 1966 and 2 April 1970.

52 See ch. 1 of *Traffic in Towns,* H.M.S.O., 1963, for a useful discussion of the inherent conflict between increasing the number of vehicles and maintaining the environment in urban areas.

53 See for example, J. H. THOMPSON *et al.,* 'Toward a geography of economic health, the case of New York State', *Annals Association of American Geographers,* 1962.

54 The literature on this topic is enormous. One useful starting point might be H. W. RICHARDSON and E. G. WEST, 'Must we always take work to the workers?' *Lloyds Bank Review,* January 1964, pp. 35–48.

55 See M. YOUNG and P. WILLMOTT, *Family and Kinship in East London,* Penguin, 1957.

56 For a lively, if polemical, discussion of speculative gains, see ch. 11 of E. CARTER, *The Future of London,* Pelican, 1962.

2 Scientific method, quantitative techniques and the teaching of geography†

In recent years there have been many changes in geography at university level, as the previous chapter shows. These have involved both content (where the emphasis has shifted from regional studies towards the study of problems concerned with the urban environment and the developing countries) and the type and range of techniques taught. Changes involving techniques have caused particular apprehension among teachers (not only at school level, it may be said) especially when the so-called new geography has been characterized – to the point of caricature – by abstruse statistical techniques. This view of the new geography is, some feel, unfair and only clouds the issue – the issue being that the rapid changes that are taking place are more important than just changes in content and techniques. They are changes in approach or method rather than content or technique. And the change which many think is at the heart of geography is that towards the use of the scientific method in approaching problems. Some would argue that it has no place, others perhaps that all geography should be based upon it. Many are undecided or uninformed. The argument will continue.

But if, as M. H. Yeates states, 'Geography can be regarded as a science concerned with the rational development and testing of theories that explain and predict the spatial distribution and location of various characteristics on the surface of the earth,'[1] then the development of theories or generalizations which may be tested or used to predict is fundamental. The term 'scientific method' is applied to the procedure by which such theories are established.

An outline of the core of the scientific method approach is given in fig. 26. With reference to fig. 26, it can be seen that the first step is the definition of a problem. The preliminary scanning of data indicates a tentative line of investigation by the realization of the presence of order in a given spatial distribution. The recording of the relevant data in some form (on maps, as a written set of data, or on computer tape, for example), allows a further analysis of the patterns developed. At this stage there may be some description in quantitative terms of the distribution being analysed. This will then allow the development of a set of hypotheses stating the possible relationship between two or more variables.

An example of this approach, used in teaching eleven-year-olds, is shown in the Stewart Farm exercise (Part 1, Unit III). Here, preliminary examination

†B. P. FitzGerald

of the mapped data leads to the formulation of the hypotheses, 'that there is an inverse relationship between the value per acre of the land and the degree of slope.' It may be said that in my experience discussion with the pupils can lead to a formal statement such as that given above, even if it is not first raised in such careful terms.

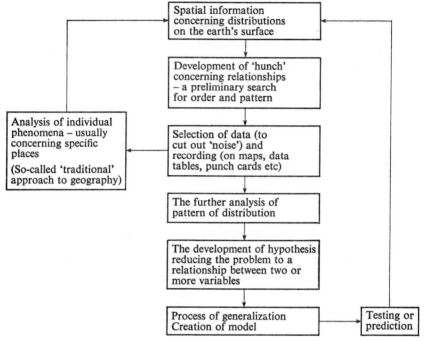

Fig 26. Comparison between the traditional method and a scientific method in geography

The two variables in this case are:

(a) the value of the land use per acre which is a *dependent variable*, dependent on

(b) the degree of slope of land, which is therefore termed the *independent variable* and which is in no way affected itself by the dependent variable.

Once such a hypothesis has been formulated it may be tested by the plotting of the values of y (the dependent variable) against x (the independent variable) on a graph as shown in fig. 27.

Note here the importance of obtaining a continuous variable, in this case the value of land per acre, rather than a discontinuous variable (e.g. type of land use) which would not otherwise lend itself to such analysis.

Reference to fig. 27 suggests that there is here a discernible 'line of dots' and therefore a fairly strong relationship between value of land per acre and the degree of slope. The significance and precise form of this relationship can be given by the statistical process of regression analysis.[2, 3, 4] In the case of the eleven-year-old group the assessment was subjective and involved no more than the drawing of an enveloping 'sausage' around the mass of dots. Reference here may be made to the various modern mathematics projects, such as the Contemporary Schools Mathematics[5] and the School Mathematics Project [6] particularly the volumes dealing with the first two years of the syllabuses. These include much material relevant to geographical work of this kind.

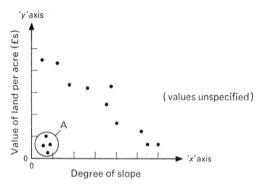

Fig 27. Graph of the relationship between the value of land and degree of slope

If a dependent variable is thought to be affected by a number of independent variables, recourse may be had to multiple regression techniques. However, although the principle is the same, computation is so laborious as to be highly impracticable even at sixth-form level, unless access to a computer is available. The type of data that would lend itself to such analysis would include intercensal population change data for settlements in an area such as East Anglia.[7]

Once the significance of a set of relationships has been established, this could lead to a generalization which in turn could be tested on similar data but in a different area. This generalization would therefore have validity if proved by testing, and could be said to be a theory. Yeates defines a theory as 'a general statement that defines and explains the inter-relationship between a number of variables,' and goes on to add that 'a tenable theory can be substantiated by empirical verification.'[8]

Many theories are, however, an integral part of a rather more structured representation of reality, normally referred to as a 'model'. Haggett and Chorley have suggested that a model 'is thus a simplified structuring of reality which presents supposedly significant features or relationships in a generalized form.' They go on to add that they 'are highly subjective approximations in that they do not include all associated observations or measurements, but as such they are valuable in obscuring incidental detail and in allowing fundamental aspects of reality to appear.'[9] Others suggest that models are essential to the generation and extension of theories and Chorley has stated that 'a model becomes a theory about the real world only when a segment of the real world has been successfully mapped into it'.[10]

Cole and King suggest that 'one of the main purposes in using models is to provide a simpler situation or one that is easier to appreciate and study than the prototype.'[11] Or as Walford puts it: 'If the basic structure of the model is understood – without all the later complexities – then the basic structure of reality may be better understood.'[12] In this way then the model (and, indeed, the construction of models) lends itself to a better understanding of the fundamental principles of an aspect of the subject.

Thus such generalizations allow the development of testable and predictive theories. Such testing allows both validation of the model or theory and also the indication of apparent anomalies which may lead to further refinement of the model. Reference to fig. 27 (and to the results of the teaching exercise on which fig. 27 is based) indicate this point. If the hypothesis shown in fig. 27 is shown to be valid as a general theory, it is possible that anomalies may appear when it is applied to specific sets of data; for example the set of readings indicated by A in fig. 27 represent one such anomalous group, investigation of which will in turn further understanding of the situation. (For further information reference should be made to the details of the Stewart Farm example.)

Of course, once model theory is found to be valid it lends itself to predictive processes. Such prediction is of utmost importance to the planner and it is a sphere in which geographers have for long been under-represented. This may have been due largely to the total failure to encourage children to predict in school.

In some instances geographers observing the workings of a geographical system have been tempted to see in them a working structure similar to that found in other sciences. In other words a pattern of activity is discernible and appears to have strong similarities with activities in, say, the physical sciences.

Model examples
Such 'working structures' or models have been the source of many important advances in social as well as physical geography. One such 'analogue' model, borrowed from physics has been the 'gravity' model which in its parent discipline is represented as:

$$I_{ij} = G \frac{M_i M_j}{(d_{ij})^2}$$

where I_{ij} is the interaction (gravitational force) between two bodies i and j
        M_i, M_j are the masses of the two bodies
        d_{ij} is the distance separating them
and G is the gravitational constant

Hypothetically it was suggested that the interaction between any neighbouring pair of settlements $(i, j,)$ would be directly proportional to the product of their size (P_i and P_j), and would be inversely proportional to the distance (d_{ij}) separating them. Thus the larger the settlements, the greater the interaction (as judged by transport frequency, telephone communications, business exchange etc.) is likely to be, but the greater the distance between them the less interaction there is likely to be. This can be written:

$$I_{ij} = \frac{P_i P_j}{(d_{ij})^2}$$ *The exponent '2' is usually included but may be varied (see below).*

This hypothesis lends itself to empirical work, and can form the basis of much experimental work carried out at sixth-form level, even by individuals carrying out their own research work.

Two examples will illustrate this.

(a) The prediction of traffic flow between centres on a main route-way (see fig. 28).

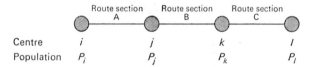

Fig 28. Settlements along a main route: the basis for calculations on the gravity model

Expected interaction between i and j (generated by i and j)

$$I_{ij} = \frac{P_i P_j}{(d_{ij})^2} \tag{1}$$

between j and k (generated by j and k)

$$I_{jk} = \frac{P_j P_k}{(d_{jk})^2} \tag{2}$$

between k and l (generated by k and l)

$$I_{kl} = \frac{P_k P_l}{(d_{kl})^2} \tag{3}$$

between i and k (generated by i and k)

$$I_{ik} = \frac{P_i P_k}{(d_{ik})^2} \tag{4}$$

between i and l (generated by i and l)

$$I_{il} = \frac{P_i P_l}{(d_{il})^2} \tag{5}$$

between j and l (generated by j and l)

$$I_{jl} = \frac{P_j P_l}{(d_{jl})^2} \tag{6}$$

The values obtained for 1, 2 ... 6 may then be placed in a simple matrix, which is no more than a convenient way to store such answers – see below.

	i	j	k	l
i	0	(1)	(4)	(5)
j		0	(2)	(6)
k			0	(3)
l				0

Note:
1 The bottom left-hand half of the matrix is just a mirror-image of the top right-hand part, and may therefore be omitted.
2 Interaction between one place and itself is assumed to be zero in terms of movement along the route.

Predicted traffic flow matrix

Each value having been placed in its appropriate 'box' in the matrix it is now possible to work out a predicted value for each section of route. (See fig. 29.) The proportion of the total traffic predicted through Route Section A will be the sum of that:

between	i and j = Value (1)
between	i and k = Value (4)
and between	i and l = Value (5)
or a Value	(1) + (4) + (5)

Likewise the proportion of the total traffic predicted through Route Section B will be the sum of that predicted:

between	i and k = Value (4)
between	j and k = Value (2)
between	j and l = Value (6)
and between	i and l = Value (5)
or a Value	(4) + (2) + (6) + (5)

Whereas the proportion of the total value for Route Section 6 can be found to be a Value (5) + (6) + (3)

The result will be a plain number for each section. This is not a prediction of actual numbers, but a prediction of a proportion of all flow. If large numbers are obtained, as is usual, these may be reduced by a convenient factor (e.g. 1,000). The reduction does not affect the result as proportionality only has to be maintained.

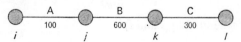

Fig 29. *Settlements along a main route: predicted flows between centres, based on the gravity model*

Thus it is predicted that section B will have twice as much traffic as section C (600:300) and six times as much traffic as A (600:100).

Once the proportions have been calculated such a model may be tested 'in the field' using traffic counts, and the validity or otherwise of the model demonstrated.

The second example leans upon a derivation of the basic gravity model, and is normally referred to as the 'breaking point' theory. The analogue here is with the breaking point or 'watershed' between the gravitational field of one body and that of another. Recent excursions between the earth and the moon illustrated the point well, as being the stage at which the space vehicle ceases decelerating on its journey from earth and commences its acceleration towards the moon. In terms of settlement geography this point would represent a point of consumer indifference. Here a consumer living between two centres would feel indifferent about visiting either of the two towns i and j. The fact that he may live at k closer to town i than town j is offset by town j being larger and offering, therefore, greater shopping opportunity (see fig. 30).

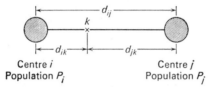

Fig 30. *Calculation of the 'breaking-point' between two centres, 'i' and 'j'*

It can be shown[11] that the distance (d_{jk}) this point of indifference (or breaking point between the urban fields of the two towns) is from centre j is:

$$d_{jk} = \frac{d_{ij}}{1 + \sqrt{\dfrac{P_i}{P_j}}}$$

In the case of an area such as the South Midlands or East Anglia the calculation of breaking points between neighbouring pairs of centres will allow the interpolation of the boundaries of urban fields as shown in fig. 31.

Once a set of urban fields has been predicted these may themselves be tested by direct questionnaire techniques applied to shoppers in each settlement, each being asked the whereabouts of his place of residence. It should be added that such work should be carried out only with the knowledge and agreement of the local planning authorities, who, in any case, may have the results of such surveys available for analysis in this way. It is strongly contended that such data, although apparently second-hand should be used, as at this level there is little to be gained by a senseless repeat of field work already done.

This method may also be used to delimit the fields of influence within the suburban area of a large city.[13]

Testing both these versions of the gravity model may produce anomalies. These, far from negating the use of the model, serve as a starting point for discussion. For instance the validity of using population figures to represent the attractive force of 'mass' may be contended. Other possibilities might include using numbers of shops in the centre (of one particular type i.e. clothing, or

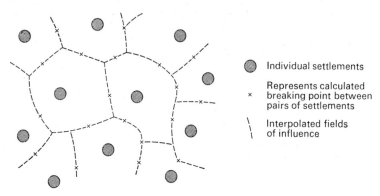

Individual settlements

× Represents calculated breaking point between pairs of settlements

\ Interpolated fields of influence

Fig 31. The construction of urban fields of influence by use of the breaking-point formula

the total), the total retail floor space, the total retail turnover (even for certain categories of goods) and so on. Some of this information may be collected in the field, other is available in planning reports such as the Enfield Report.[14] On the other hand it may be that mileage distance is an unreal concept of space to use. Would it be more realistic to use time distance? Indeed, what effect is produced by lines of communication which decrease the 'friction of distance' between centres? Should the exponent of d (distance) be 2, or should it be 1, or some intermediate value? What does this exponent represent in terms of friction of distance? Would it be very different if one compared, say Ghana, England and the United States?

Quantitative methods

Little has been said so far about abstruse statistics and mathematics. Their place in new geography is often exaggerated. But it is of course most helpful to have some idea of the usefulness of mathematics. After all geography is a spatial science, so that spatial geometries must play a part. For example, the mathematician's ideas concerning space may well be of direct relevance here. A whole brand of mathematics deals with 'rubber sheet' geometry or topology which has a very real bearing on geography. In topology little emphasis is placed on distance, straightness and orientation, and more important are order and contiguity. Reference here may be made to Cole and King (1968),[15] Chorley and Haggett (1967),[16] Haggett (1965),[17] *Schools Mathematics Project Book 2*[18] and *Contemporary Schools Mathematics*.[19] Particularly important here is the idea that space may be transformed, and so create a different base upon which distributions may be observed and patterns revealed for the first time. Such space transformations might involve transformation into time or cost space, income space and so on. Cost and time transformations worked at fourth- and sixth-form levels with data from British Rail is given in Everson and FitzGerald (1969),[20] and interesting examples of transformation into income and population space are given in Haggett (1965) [21] where reference is made to the transformation of a part of Tacoma (USA) into income space by Getis, and to the transformation of southern England into a population space map based on the voting population of electoral districts in 1964.

One other aspect of mathematics already referred to is statistics. Much new geography has been maligned because of its supposed heavy reliance upon statistical techniques. Of course statistics are important, and Cole and King suggest that they fall into three broad categories. The first is purely descriptive and does no more than describe a set of data numerically, so as to express meaningfully its magnitude and spread. Such statistics deal with measures of central tendency (mean, median and mode) and dispersion or spread (e.g. standard deviation, skewness). The second involves sampling, as one often needs to base hypotheses on data that does not cover the whole population. Such a process may require random, regular or stratified sampling and some idea of the significance of the sample taken. The third involves inferential statistics, whereby the significance of the correlation between variables may be tested. An outline of such methods may be found in Cole and King,[22] and a fuller account in Moroney [23] and Gregory.[24]

Statistical analysis itself is not dealt with exhaustively here, not only because it is much better dealt with elsewhere, but also because many techniques have assumed an unnecessarily prominent role in recent changes in geographical approach. In a teaching situation, although it is important to emphasize a need for precision, it is important to choose statistical techniques that both suit the task in hand and the level of attainment of the pupil concerned.

References

1 M. H. YEATES, *An Introduction to Quantitative Analysis in Economic Geography*, McGraw-Hill, 1968, p. 1.

2 S. GREGORY, *Statistical Methods and the Geographer*, Longman, 1963, ch. 12.

3 M. J. MORONEY, *Facts from Figures*, Penguin, 1951, chs. 16 and 19.

4 A. J. SHERLOCK, *An Introduction to Probability and Statistics*, Arnold, 1962.

5 A. J. SHERLOCK, *Contemporary School Mathematics*; a series of textbooks and topic books leading to O-level, Arnold.

6 A. J. SHERLOCK, *The School Mathematics Project*, a series of textbooks leading to O- and A-levels, C.U.P.

7 J. A. EVERSON and B. P. FITZGERALD, *Settlement Patterns,* Longman, 1969, ch. 5.

8 YEATES, *op. cit.,* pp. 3–4.

9 R. J. CHORLEY and P. HAGGETT, eds., *Models in Geography,* Methuen, 1967, p. 22.

10 R. J. CHORLEY, 'Geography and analogue theory', *Annals of the Association of American Geographers,* Vol. 54, pp. 127–137.

11 J. P. COLE and C. A. M. KING, *Quantitative Geography,* Wiley, 1968, p. 464.

12 R. A. WALFORD, *Games in Geography,* Longman, 1969.

13 J. A. EVERSON and B. P. FITZGERALD, *Inside the City,* Longman, 1972.

14 London Borough of Enfield Report on Shopping.

15 COLE and KING, *op. cit.,* pp. 85–93.

16 CHORLEY and HAGGETT, *op. cit.,* ch. 15.

17 P. HAGGETT, *Locational Analysis in Human Geography,* Arnold, 1965, pp. 65–67.

18 P. HAGGETT, *The School Mathematics Project,* Book 2, *op. cit.*

19 J. C. REYNOLDS, 'Shape, Size and Place', part of the *Contemporary School Mathematics* books, *op. cit.*

20 EVERSON and FITZGERALD, *Settlement Patterns, op. cit.,* ch. 11.

21 P. HAGGETT, *Locational Analysis in Human Geography, op. cit.,* ch. 2.

22 COLE and KING, *op. cit.,* ch. 3.

23 MORONEY, *op. cit.,* various references throughout.

24 GREGORY, *op. cit.,* various references throughout.

3 Models, simulations and games†

The uninvolved sometimes seem to assume that the most important new development in geography over the last twenty years has been the 'quantitative revolution'. It is at any rate quantitative work that bears the brunt of much of the criticism levelled against new developments. From the other side of the fence, however, most new geographers see the pattern in rather less restricted terms. David Harvey in *Explanations in Geography*[1] has been one of the most recent to express this, in pointing out how his own early enchantment with methods of quantitative analysis was later to be much changed by the realization of a more fundamental movement in modern geography – the development of a more rigorous and scientific approach, as described by Brian Fitzgerald in chapter 2.

This change in methodology has had several consequences. One major development is generally conceded to be the use and development of the model – a term which has at once become both the darling and the monster to different generations of geographers.

In Britain, the model's metamorphosis since the sand-tray and papier-mache era has been achieved largely by one weighty volume, *Models in Geography*, edited by Chorley and Haggett[2] the second of the series which put the summer Madingley seminars on the lasting geographical map. The 816 pages and 2000 references were heady wine to some, undrinkable brew to others. A reviewer in the *Geographical Journal* wrote:

> . . . in retrospect, a turning point in the development of geographical methodology in Britain. After the exploratory and mildly iconoclastic contents of the first Madingley lectures, recorded in *Frontiers in Geographical Teaching*, a more substantial statement of the methodological basis and aims of the so-called 'new geography' was urgently required . . . With the publication of this book, (it is demonstrated that) the traditional classificatory paradigm is inadequate and that in the context of the 'new geography' an irreversible step has been taken to push us back into the mainstream of scientific activity by way of the uncomfortable and highly-specialized process of model building. The discussion of the relevance of new conceptual models in geographical research and teaching should serve as a stimulus to participation in methodological debate to which, with notable exceptions, British geographers have made a disproportionately small contribution. It is therefore a major publication, both in achievement and potential.[3]

† Rex Walford

A reviewer in the journal which most teachers read, *Geography*, was less enamoured, however:

> What . . . is its object, and to whom is it addressed? These questions are avoided with perverse skill and in the absence of guidance, the conviction gradually takes root that, in fact, the authors are writing for each other! This may explain, though it does not excuse, the use in some papers of a barbarous and repulsive jargon. Is it then a joint expression of faith on the part of the New Geographers? This would indeed have been welcome but a new faith is hardly likely to be attained by a frenzied search through the realms of physical and social science for gadgets which might conceivably be turned to geographical ends. The nature of those ends calls for solid thought, a task which cannot be delegated to computers.[4]

Such high feeling was an indication of the controversy which the book raised, and indeed still raises. But some observers have considered this to be a necessary agony, a prelude to change of fundamental importance.

> Really significant revolution in ideas stem not from relatively minor changes carried out within the conceptual framework of the age but from what Thomas Kuhn would call the creation of a new paradigm. It is a change of paradigm which I believe to be taking place in geography . . . The model is proposed as a likely means of integrating hitherto disparate geographical traditions. A model-based paradigm is envisaged as replacing the old predominantly classificatory geographical tradition . . . I agree 100% with the thesis of this work in its implicit assumption that geographical study at all levels is in need of, and is fortunately being provided with, new categories of thought. *And this means a break with the past.*[5]

Wheatley goes on to suggest that new categories will not only affect research, but will have repercussions too throughout the geographical world. He postulates that modifications will overcome the school examination boards (whom he calls, perhaps a trifle unkindly, 'that last bastion of geographical conservatism') and that finally changes will occur in the school classrooms themselves.

I am a little upset that he sees the classroom at the end of the line. One would have thought that changes in the classroom might be a necessary preliminary to changes in the examination system if enthusiastic and creative teachers are in fact making any contribution to the organization and development of syllabuses. Wheatley's supposition is that change will be brought to the examination boards by their university members; I find this a sad comment on the present situation. It is true, however, that by no means all teachers would agree with Wheatley's analysis of the significance of new geography; nor perhaps would they agree with his suggestion of inevitable repercussions.

Since this paper is connected basically with the significance of model theory for classroom teaching, it is to this that I now turn. It may be helpful to look first at some of the obstacles and barriers which have been set up, and to consider the arguments for completely ignoring the whole thing in schools.

One view postulates that whatever the significance of model theory for academic geographers in the universities, the approach is a blind alley as far as school teaching is concerned. New geographical techniques and investigations are stigmatized as recondite or even as 'attempted only for prestige', and not thought to be relevant to the on-going task of getting through a double-period with 3C. This potentially divisive idea already has its proponents in those who seek no relationship between geography taught at primary and secondary level (a fact which has in many cases allowed primary school geography to slip further and further into the pursuit of antique tribes and animals); and to want a relationship does not imply that one teaches in a school in which all geographers are potentially university candidates.

The need for unity within the subject is more than a practical one of preparing sixth-formers for their first lectures on campus; it is, I would assert, a basic requirement for the continued existence of that subject in any coherent way. This point was recently made by Cooke and Johnson in their preface to *Trends in Geography*,[6] a book designed to serve the middle-ground between universities and schools in relating modern developments to teachers and students.

> Techniques of study are changing more rapidly in modern geography than at any previous time in the subject's history. As a result there is a great need for a dialogue between research workers and those being admitted to the mysteries of the subject. Teachers provide the necessary link; and it is dangerous for the vitality and future health of geography that some teachers find current developments either incomprehensible or unacceptable.

The danger that they mention is, one suspects, born from the feeling that the geographical train exists as a unit and that carriages cannot be detached into sidings without some lasting effect on the efficiency of the total unit.

It might be more positive to realize that the sensitivity to current problems which draws academic geography into new methodology and techniques is merely an indication of changing circumstances for the subject as a whole; the experience of the scouts and the frontiersmen is surely an indication to those who are driving the educational wagon-trains.

A second obstacle to the adoption of model theory has been a semantic one. The 'barbarous and repulsive jargon' already mentioned may be seen by its originators as an aid towards more precise clarification of thought, but there is no doubt that some already daunted by new ideas use the excuse of new language to withdraw altogether.

Model building, locational analysis and the new scientific rigour in geography have instituted a fresh vocabulary in many cases; fresh, that is, to traditional geographers. The language of systems analysis, for instance, frequently used by locationalists to explain the dynamic nature of models, is not one that geographers have previously known with any expertise. 'Feedback', 'linkages' and other such terms are confusing and unfamiliar. Systems analysis has, nevertheless, provided a lingua franca, a common bond with other disciplines, and it is precisely because of this adoption that geographers have reasserted themselves in such inter-disciplinary studies as regional science and urban studies. Systems approaches are not strange to sociologists, economists, town and regional planners or engineers, and geographers have become significantly better equipped to take on conversation with such groups when given a systems grounding. It is at least possible that there might be an analagous result in schools, although it is clear that other subjects experience similar difficulties at present in linking academic and classroom methodologies.

In one particular case apparent flippancy, in addition to unfamiliarity has proved a semantic obstacle. Gould himself pointed out the problem of using the word 'game' in relation to an environmental situation in which some elements of conflict or competition were apparent, and some have advocated that this major part of model theory should be dignified with some grander title in order to cut down on the ribald comments. Luckily, the word seems to have assumed more respectable connotations at a strategic time. Eric Berne's popular study of human behaviour described 'games people play'[7] and saw much of life in game situations. More relevantly to geographers, Nigel Calder has written of the general struggle of man and environment in similar terms[8].

> Let there be no mistake about it – a game there must be. Human and material resources have to be deployed according to some set of rules. Men want a sense of purpose in their lives, something they know they must do when they get up in the morning, and a means of measuring their achievement by some objective criterion at the end of the day . . . So while, by talking of 'games', we recognize the ephemeral character of social institutions that seem obsessively indispensable to those in the thick of the old game, we need not be cynical in our use of the word.

A third kind of objection to the adoption of model theory in the classroom has come from those who see an obsessive theorizing setting in as a result of it. The battle of the previous age was the battle to make geography real – to liberate it from the aridity of textbook description and to take it into the concrete environment. In Briault's immortal epigram, 'Off with the gown and on with the raincoat; away with the chalk and on with the boots; for through the soles of the feet shall ye learn.'

Does concern with models, theories and ideas suggest that the battle almost won is about to be thrown away? I think (and a following paper bears out) that quite the reverse is true. Those most concerned with the development of models have not only been clearly interested in field work as well as classroom work in schools; they have also been instrumental in improving the standard and the satisfaction gained from such work. Model-building may be seen as an aid to a more structured and purposeful approach to the environment, and field work may come to be used in a much more integrated way as a result of it.

To observe before theorizing leads not only to inefficient observation but also to uncertain conclusions because no specific idea has been identified or tested. To theorize before observing forces the observer to think through the processes that may be at work, focuses the attention on a manageable number of ideas and limits the observation to selected phenomena only. This seems to be not dissimilar to the differences between the approaches of regional geography and spatial analysis.[9]

Field-work investigations clearly do not accompany the investigation of settlement patterns in Brazil or industrial locations in Australia; but they may well be given depth and direction when the more general topics of, say, the central business district or transport networks come up for study and can be satisfactorily illustrated by data drawn from local case studies.

But more fundamentally, some would object, concentration on models is an antithesis to the real world; what children need to feel and experience are the sample and case studies of real life rather than theories engineered in the cause of internal consistency at the expense of reality. Such a view seems to misunderstand the nature of reality itself, models seek not only to generalize, but to act as a guide to the reality *not* readily seen – the network of shopping or commuting patterns in a town, for instance, as distinct from its more easily observed bricks and mortar – and in this they can be valuable paths to understanding of what is not observable. Perhaps one should add that models are certainly being misused if their developers and users do not concern themselves with their reapplicability to the real world and to particular sets of phenomena around which they have been developed.

A fourth objection to models is made by those who see them as interesting playthings for the high-flyers but of no real relevance to the early school-leaver or Newsom child in the secondary school. Models are very difficult things to understand, so the argument runs; the pupils will not grasp the ideas of hypothesis and generality, and in any case this is not the kind of geography that we want them to be learning. They need to be prepared for the basics of life, and to go out informed in a general way about the concrete nature of the world in which they live.

This particular argument might be stronger if we could find many examples of satisfactory pieces of geography learning in this sphere. However much evidence suggests that the Newsom child, like his cleverer brother, usually remembers only a fragmentary tissue of the information given to him at school. He recalls perhaps the bizarre story of Krakatoa because of its gory disasters, or the mnemonic about 'wet windy winters and short sharp summers', or curiously stores the colourful information that there are liquorice fields west of Pontefract. But our normal fare for him is only a less rigorous variant of the factual information fed to the GCE stream. The cascading fountain of data that a teacher has to cope with seems to be in little danger of drying up. In fact, there is no doubt that the flow is increasing in intensity and that the value of any geographical fact becomes that bit more transitory every year.

Faced with this, the attempt to show process and system by the use of a model that simplifies reality seems to me to be a hopeful possibility for even the less able forms. Current educational research suggests moreover that we may have to re-think our normal grading of children's abilities. The GCE form may be compounded of those with efficient data-storage facilities, rather than those with genuine agility of mind or even intuitive understanding.

Models do not have to be complex, jargon-riddled or impossibly mathematical. There can be simple kinds of role-play exercise or operational game, in which simple and basic ideas are set working. It is sad if model experiment is always concentrated in the more able forms of schools. One can imagine, for instance, that Cole and Beynon's *New Ways in Geography*,[10] intended for primary schools – might be more useful to 1C or 2C than the 1937 editions of somebody's round-the-world geography.

Even if objections such as these are mistaken, it remains for a positive case to be put for the adoption of model theory in schools. And in any case, you may be thinking, what exactly does it mean in classroom terms?

Chorley and Haggett's definition of a model is important, and probably definitive in terms of British experience, and so it is worth examining it as a preliminary to any further consideration. They say:

> The most fundamental feature of models is that their construction has involved a highly selective attitude to information, wherein not only 'noise' but 'less important signals' have been eliminated to enable one to see something of the heart of things. Models can be viewed as *selective approximations which, by the elimination of incidental detail, allow some fundamental relevant or interesting aspects of the real world to appear in some generalized form.*[11]

This 'selective attitude to information' is clearly relevant to a world of exploding data like ours. The suggestion is that the model can represent the important aspects of a process or system to the exclusion of less important ones. It can be static or dynamic. But it is important for the learning process that the model is also a structured vehicle. To quote Chorley and Haggett again, 'the selected significant aspects of the web of reality are exploited in terms of their connections.'[12]

By now, we have all read a little Bruner, and so may know that crucial passage where he points out:

> the curriculum of a subject should be determined by the most fundamental understanding that can be achieved of the underlying principles that give

structure to that subject. Teaching specific topics or skills without making clear their context in the broader fundamental structure of a field of knowledge is uneconomical in several deep senses.

In the first place, such teaching makes it exceedingly difficult for the student to generalize from what he has learned to what he will encounter later. In the second place, learning that has fallen short of a grasp of general principles has little reward in terms of intellectual excitement. The best way to create interest in a subject is to render it worth knowing, which means to make the knowledge gained usable in one's thinking beyond the situation in which the learning has occurred. Third, knowledge one has acquired without sufficient structure to tie it together is knowledge that is likely to be forgotten. An unconnected set of facts has a pitiably short life in the memory. Organizing facts in terms of principles and ideas from which they may be inferred is the only known way of reducing the quick rate of loss of human memory.[13]

I judge these to be powerful arguments in favour of study in depth, and study of process and structure. It is encouraging to read a few pages later in Bruner how he saw a demonstration in which fifth-grade children rapidly grasped central ideas from the theory of functions by means of a game, i.e. a concrete operation in Piaget's terms, even though the formal explanation of the ideas would not have meant much to them. It is an encouragement to take model-building into the practical sphere. If this is done, then model-building and model-operating become communal occupations in the classroom. The terms 'simulation' and 'operational game' are used alongside the more general title in this context. It would appear, from what little experience we have, that such building and operating make a highly enjoyable and motivating experience for most pupils. This is a delightful, but accidental, bonus to the use of models in geography teaching, since we should still be pursuing the possibilities if they were dull and difficult.

Even in a comparatively short time, a variety of styles and approaches have developed, and it is the purpose of the latter part of this paper to consider some of these briefly, particularly in relation to dynamic models, i.e., simulation and games.

Some classroom material was being developed in the United States in the early 1960s and the officially sponsored American High School Geography Project was certainly a pioneer in this field. The A.H.S.G.P. produced a variety of model ideas in its experimental trials, and even though the final work of the project has only recently been published,[14] its Metfab and Portsville models of industrial location and town growth are much-quoted examples. There has also been a good deal of simulation material produced by Social Studies Curriculum Projects in the States, though some of this is designed for therapy and empathy, rather than for the understanding of particular ideas. Certain community problems at school-, class or town-level are designed in model situations, and class participation in the development of these has been seen to provide useful positive experience. In Britain, the pamphlet by J. P. Cole and G. A. Smith on 'Geographical Games' put many people on to basic ideas in the mid-1960s,[15] and some of these were later developed in the Cole and Beynon series of concept-dominated textbooks for primary schools.[16] Other work was done by individual teachers working partly from scraps of information gleaned transatlantically or via university departments, partly from intuition and a keen eye for what was genuinely successful in the classroom.

One might usefully, though quite roughly, divide the material currently available to teachers into four main types:

(a) Role-playing exercises
These are fairly informally designed models in which equipment is rarely if ever used, and in which structure is implanted only at the beginning of the situation. The development of such an exercise usually involves the creation of a particular situation (hypothetical or based on reality) and the briefing of players concerning it. Players are then briefed about the particular roles that they will simulate, either by biographical note, or by general oral instruction.

The operation of the model situation is then in the hands of the players. If they are simulating a town council taking a decision about a new shopping centre, they are free, working from their given base, to develop the argument in any way that seems suitable. Such models clearly give major importance to the instincts, irrationalities and individual traits of human behaviour in exploring how decisions are made. They also provide a useful way of showing, in a simplified manner, how the actual clash of human personality is an important factor in the development of situations. Decisions with geographical implications – the siting of a shopping precinct, the routing of a by-pass – are hardly ever pure geographical decisions, and the role-playing exercises emphasize the importance of understanding human behaviour and of acting with strategy, diplomacy and tact, even though you are sure that you are right.

Some of these exercises have been used in colleges and schools, and a recent BBC geography series, designed for CSE pupils, relied heavily on the role-playing exercise for follow-up work.[17] One BBC education officer, visiting a fourth-year class reported: 'I had a quick try-out of the follow-up on the programme about the Holme Pierpoint power station site. It went surprisingly well and I am sure the producer is on to a good thing here.' He also reported how, in a small rural secondary school, a teacher had followed up the programmes. 'Discussion and argument, often carrying over into English lessons, had been commonplace. The class had their own parish meeting on a hypothetical water crisis. The water crisis programme fitted in very neatly with a local studies project which they had recently done on their own water supply.'

(b) Mathematical models
In contrast to this, some models emphasize the complete randomness of chance factors in a more clinical way. The use of random numbers tables, of

dice or of some other chance mechanism may be part of a purely mathematical operation in relation to the model structure.

The many diffusion models, based on the Hagerstrand 'Monte Carlo' simulation,[18] for example, rely on the model-builder to evaluate the attractiveness of areas and then to rely on random numbers to generate the pattern of diffusion. Thus squares near the original generation point are usually more likely to receive some early transmission, squares separated from the original generation point by some physical or cultural barrier are under-favoured, and so on. Such a diffusion model has been used, in my knowledge, to generate such different patterns as the spread of cream-separators in South Africa and the spread of a passing craze for yo-yos in a primary school.

A second example of this kind of mathematical model is provided by the model of town growth, demonstrated by D. E. Keeble in the January 1969 issue of *Geography*.[9] Here, the model makes the tacit assumption that the role-playing of countless individuals over a hundred year period is clearly impossible, but that their general pattern of decision can be simulated by a combination of environmental and stochastic factors. This development of stochastic (chance) techniques has been one of the major lessons learnt from other social sciences, and it has helped to rid us of the last vestiges of old-style determinism. Whether it introduces a new-style determinism in its place, is a point that some would wish to argue.

(c) Individual exercises

Not all models involve group work. It is entirely practical for particular situations to be developed so that individuals are confronted with purely personal decisions about the development and operation of certain simulated events.

The often-quoted exercise about town-siting, developed in the first (urban based) unit of the American High School Project is a good example. Here the student is confronted with a set of maps of the physical environment and a collection of alternative sites for settlement. He is asked to evaluate them, according to the historical date given to him for each map. At the end of this evaluation, he makes a personal decision, as would the autocratic leader of any group of founding settlers. Such an individual exercise allows the comparison of answers – though it should be emphasized that it is hardly wise for one answer to be thought right simply because the majority choose it.

This particular approach to model-theory seems deceptively simple, but there is a difference between a pupil who reads site or route characteristics in his textbook, and one who is placed in a position where he is forced to consider them for himself. It is certainly likely that this approach has been practised by many teachers for years, though perhaps without being dignified with the name 'simulation' or 'model'. Every sample study in which the teacher urges pupils to 'put themselves in the place of the farmer' has the vital elements, every essay written from the point of view of the deckhand on the trawler or the schoolboy in the foreign country has at least the germ of simulation in it.

(d) Operational games

Whereas the role-play may involve the whole class in a corporate decision and the individual exercise may involve only one pupil in a private debate with himself, the operational game is usually seen as a half-way house between the two.

The elements of such a model involve the simulation of situations where there is an element of conflict or competition between groups, or between a group and the environment, or between alternative strategies. Gould's original paper on game theory postulated the problem in terms of the game that African farmers eternally played against the environment[20] and a succession of farm games has followed up that pattern.[21] The possibilities of rival railway companies building routes across a continent, or of developers and preservationists indulging in a battle over a rural landscape have similar elements of conflict and can be seen as a game situation. It is possible to list some fifteen or twenty activities of basic interest to geographers in which a similar situation can be discerned. These activities can be usefully divided into those concerned with points (e.g. locational decisions concerning towns or factories), lines (e.g. routing problems of air, road, rail) or surfaces (e.g. transformation of land areas, reclamation of deserts). Fig. 32 explains this further.

Such games do not by any means assume that profit is the ultimate motive, nor do they make any comment about the nature of a competitive world. They seek to describe the world as they find it, and to model existing situations in order that they may be better understood. The operational game, whether involving equipment or not, in my experience has considerable potential in the classroom, since most children beyond the age of nine are no strangers to the art of game playing. Often, in their concern to improve the game and make it more realistic. they come very close to the exact intentions of the teacher, who wants them to see its relationship to reality.

In these four general categories there is already a considerable amount of material. More is being produced and tested, adopted and rejected, each month.

It is important that enthusiastic model builders recall a further point made by Chorley and Haggett, that 'most geographical model builders would judge the value of a model almost entirely in terms of its re-applicability to the real world.'[22] There may be a temptation to play happily with something which keeps the class occupied but which has step by step moved farther from reality. The model in the classroom must always be carefully de-briefed and integrated into more orthodox teaching, or else the arguments about its fantasy and irrelevance may well become justified. It is also salutary to remember that methodology should not be the guiding hand in the development of the curriculum. However successful models of various kinds appear to

Activity relating to **lines**   Activity relating to **points**

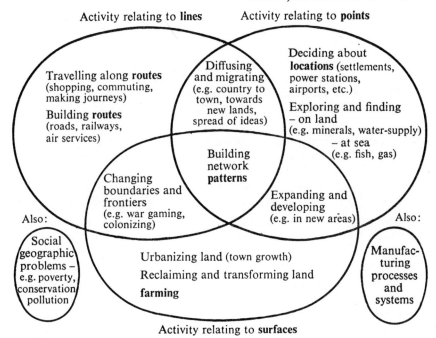

Fig 32. A model of dynamic themes in geography: a basis for the identification of topics for games.

be, techniques should not run wild without a sense of direction. The use of these models must be determined by our ultimate concern in the objectives of the syllabus.

I think it no accident that in terms of syllabus, process and system activity of various kinds seems to be coming more important – and thus the tide runs for models at present. The value of models however lies not in their mere existence but in their contribution to a total curriculum pattern. To some, they seem strange and unusual intruders. But if curriculum change is imminent they may become useful and trusted guides into the future pattern of geography, one that can be viable in the seventies. Past patterns are unlikely to be helpful in a world changing, liberating and developing as fast as ours is.

References

1 D. HARVEY, *Explanations in Geography,* Arnold, 1969, p. vi.

2 R. J. CHORLEY and P. HAGGETT, *Models in Geography,* Methuen, 1967.

3 O. SLAYMAKER, *Geographical Journal,* September 1968, Vol. 134, Part 2.

4 'P.R.C.', *Geography,* November 1968, Vol. 53, Part 4.

5 P. WHEATLEY, *The Bloomsbury Geographer,* 1968, University College, London, Vol. 1, No. 1.

6 R. COOKE and J. H. JOHNSON, *Trends in Geography,* Pergamon, 1969.

7 E. BERNE, *Games People Play,* Penguin, 1964.

8 N. CALDER, *The Environment Game*, Secker & Warburg (later reprinted as a Panther Science paperback), 1969, pp. 144–145 of Panther edition.

9 J. A. EVERSON, 'Some aspects of teaching geography through fieldwork', *Geography*, January 1969, Vol. 54, Part 1.

10 J. P. COLE and N. J. BEYNON, *New Ways in Geography, Introductory Book, Book I, Book II, Book III* and *Teacher's Book*, Blackwell, 1969–72.

11 CHORLEY and HAGGETT, *op. cit.*, p. 23.

12 CHORLEY and HAGGETT, *op. cit.*, p. 23.

13 J. S. BRUNER, *The Process of Education*, Random House, 1960, p. 31.

14 *Geography in an Urban Age*, the American High School Geography Project, Units I–VI, Collier-Macmillan, 1971. (Angus Gunn, writing in the *Journal of Curriculum Studies*, May 1971, Vol. 3, No. 1, points out that simulation material comprised only twenty per cent of the first three units of the Project but its ratings amongst both teachers and pupils were impressive and so the final three units had up to fifty per cent of their material simulation based.)

15 J. P. COLE and G. A. SMITH, *Bulletin of quantitative data for geographers*, No. 8, University of Nottingham, Department of Geography, 1967.

16 COLE and BEYNON, *op. cit.*

17 Teacher's notes for 'Changing Britain' BBC TV series, summer term 1969.

18 For a discussion of this see HARVEY's chapter in *Models in Geography*, *op. cit.*, especially pp. 582–592.

19 D. KEEBLE, 'School teaching and urban geography; some new approaches', *Geography*, January 1969, Vol. 54, Part 1.

20 P. GOULD, 'Man against the environment; a game-theoretic framework', *Annals of the Association of American Geographers* 53, 1963. Also reprinted in P. J. AMBROSE, ed, *Analytical Human Geography*, Longman, 1970.

21 See for instance the 'Herefordshire Farm Game' of W. V. TIDSWELL, printed in *Geography for Primary Schools*, Geographical Association, 1970.

22 CHORLEY and HAGGETT, *op., cit.*, p. 24.

4 Field work in school geography†

The difficulties that face anyone attempting work in the field in geography, or any other subject, are legion and daunting. The organizer has to find time to organize and prepare for the trip; to justify to himself and, more importantly, to others the loss of actual school teaching time, especially for classes preparing for public examinations; to find suitable staff for the work, to keep the costs down while perhaps travelling and staying in an area suitable for the type of study he wants to complete, and so on. Yet in spite of these and many other problems the amount of work attempted each year outside the classroom rises steadily. Most schools these days take their children out for some work, most syllabuses include references to possible field trips and most teachers subscribe to the view that children's work in the field can be very valuable. Further evidence for this growth can be seen in the increase recently of places that can be used as centres for longer field trips. The YHA, the Forestry Commission, the Holiday Fellowship, the LEAs and some schools and colleges all provide accommodation which can be hired and which is suitable for use as a base for field trips. Publishers have also contributed to the growth of field work by producing many books on the subject recently. These books provide much information on suitable areas, places to stay, techniques to use and above all on reasons for doing field work. But in general they neglect any discussion of the methodology of the subject.

How then is the work attempted in the field to be organized? What are the underlying objectives, and what structure of study is presumed consciously or unconsciously by the organizer? There appear to be two main philosophies. The first, perhaps the older and the English approach, could be called field work, field studies, or field teaching. The second, perhaps the newer and a more American tradition, could be called field research, to distinguish it from the other tradition.

The first approach implies to our generation of geographers, the pioneering work of such distinguished geographers as S. W. Wooldridge, particularly his collection of field excursions described in *London's Countryside*, L. D. Stamp and his work in producing the First Land Utilization Survey of Great Britain, and the efforts of organizations such as the Le Play Society. It is a tradition very firmly rooted in English geography and its underlying thought may be described in a simple flow diagram.

†John Everson

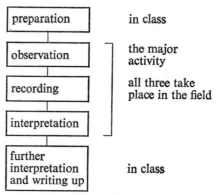

Fig 33. A traditional approach to field work

A piece of work organized in this way can vary from one with slight preparation, that will allow the students some personal discovery, to one so didactic as to make children respond to questions which guide them directly to a view of the area. The teacher may have done all his work beforehand in preparing assignments, work cards, questionnaires etc., so that he will take a less dominant role in the day's events, or he may want to teach directly in the field by lecturing or initiating discussion at certain predetermined places.

It may be valuable to look in more detail at the different stages of this approach. As I have said the amount of preparation may vary from teacher to teacher but that some preparatory work will be done is certain. This preparation may include studies of land use maps, historical maps, census returns, the various scale maps of the Ordnance Survey, suitable text books, air photographs, handouts, etc. to provide some background material for the student before he ventures into the field.

The next stage, observation alone, is at the heart of this approach. Briault and Shave in *Geography in and out of School* said 'Good field work is accurate observation, accurately recorded.'[1] In this stage the children explore an area so that they can then look at the landscape with greater insight and with a fresh eye.

Often the study will involve reaching and perhaps climbing to a good viewpoint. Box Hill or Leith Hill at once come to mind. Once there, the student will look at the countryside. Only then will he take out his map to compare the map with the reality seen around. Discussion on the spot may begin, or the teacher may comment on what is seen and guide the children in their perception of the landscape. It is said concerning this stage that the 'feature of good field teaching is to restrict the discussion to that which is visible.'

The recording of what is seen can be done in a variety of ways. The child can add to a map already provided or which he draws himself information such as river cliff, spur, flood plain, incised meander, type of hedge, age of building, type of stone used. He can also draw the landscape to show the salient features that can be seen, in a way first popularized and demonstrated by Hutchings in his work and in his book *Landscape Drawing*.[2] Notes can be written about significant features, sketch maps can be drawn, questionnaires can be answered and transects can be completed. And of course the child can just observe the landscape.

Much of the interpretation will be carried out at the same time as the observation and recording, by the very process of deciding what is important in the landscape and what should be written down or drawn. The discussion and talk by the leader will also have pointed to various interpretations which could emerge from the observed data. However, the student on return to the classroom may add to his original recordings, write them out again and generally tidy up and complete what he has done.

The results of this process will almost certainly be an increase in the motivation of the student, but whether the underlying objective – the development of what might be called an 'eye for the country' – is achieved is much harder to assess. This attribute, the ability to see and relate important components of the landscape, is thought by some exponents of this approach to be an art and consequently even harder to teach and assess. One may conclude by quoting S. W. Wooldridge who said that 'real field work is the close examination and analysis in the field of an accessible piece of country showing one or more aspects of real differentiation'.[3]

Perhaps some comment may now be made on the implications of this approach. Basic to it is the idea that somehow the totality of an area can be comprehended. When the complexities of the patterns of the landscape and the very complex underlying causal factors are considered, it seems a grandiose aim to try to understand the entire landscape presented to the viewer. This approach can very easily degenerate into the attempt at a complete regional survey of, say, a parish or a small town, where the only structure to the information presented is a chronological one, ranging from the pre-Cambrian, via the introduction of gas lighting, to the present-day land-use map. In many of the studies seen there is a heavy bias towards the physical features that appear to dominate the visible landscape. In *Teaching Geography* Long and Roberson say:

> The scene should first be broken into major components, and relief or land forms will probably be the basis of this. At a later stage, attention to detail of the major land form should not be forgotten. Against this physical background the vegetational or agricultural pattern can be placed and relationships between the two sought.[4]

Relationships can of course always be discovered if they are sought, and if the experiment is constructed so that results obtained cannot be properly tested. A further problem of this approach is that some areas such as eastern Essex (which is not considered in *London's Countryside*), are thought of as far too difficult to be studied at the child's level. This attitude has extended into

the urban area and has resulted, until very recently, in the neglect of the difficult problem landscapes presented by the town. The concentration of this approach on what can be seen i.e. land use, results in the omission, when considering rural landscapes, of factors such as where the railway leads to and the
frequency of service, agricultural subsidies, freight rate charges, urban
markets, planning, population densities. In urban areas there is again the
concentration on the skyscape or the actual buildings, and a corresponding
neglect of factors such as market thresholds, commuting, rateable values,
planning controls. Some would also say that this extreme concentration on
observation is a primary-school activity and not one that can enter into the
secondary schools almost as an end in itself. On the other hand, at the end of

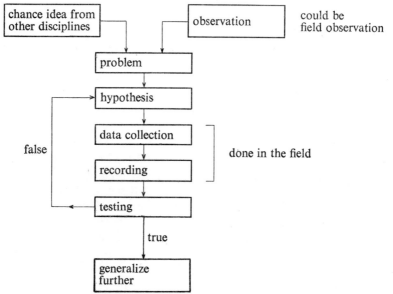

Fig 34. A field research approach

several pieces of work organized in this way there may come an appreciation of
the landscape in its broadest sense. It may be that to encourage certain desirable attitudes such as conservation or planning the child should follow this
approach. Again there is no denying that at the end of such a trip the child
may have experienced a thrill or a glimpse of something which may lead him
on to deeper and wiser studies.

The second approach, field research (see fig. 34), may be considered to have
these stages. The observational stage could of course be the descriptive approach described earlier. Equally well the piece of work might be initiated by
some idea that could enter from almost anywhere. Or classroom discussion
could have thrown up problems which the class would like to solve. The problems considered important and relevant will, of course, vary with the age,

background and geographical experience of the students, as will the hypotheses that they will want to consider as possible answers to the problem. Here then the initial stages of the approach will be in the classroom not the field. Data collection will be considered in two ways. Firstly, in the light of the problem. Information will be sought relevant only to this problem and there will be no attempt to view the entire area or landscape. Secondly, depending on the expertise of the students, some form of sampling may be introduced to gather the data needed quickly. The recording of the data could be in many ways similar to the methods described earlier, but more refined methods such as histograms, matrices or punched cards could be introduced to cater for the more sophisticated data gathered in this approach. The testing will again vary according to the need and the students' expertise. At one level it may be just the comparison of two distribution maps of, say, population and woodland, and the drawing of conclusions. At another, testing may be made by using simple ranking techniques. At another, with suitable calculating machines, regression techniques may be adopted. When the results of the tests are known, the student can, if the hypothesis was false, try again or, if it was correct, can test it further and then use his work as the basis for further generalizations.

Many geographers would be worried by this approach, feeling that it might develop an eye for a problem not an eye for country, arguing that the proper study of geography is space and not problems. It might also be argued that in many studies the children will be engaged in studying, recording and testing minutiae, as it is very difficult to test complex hypotheses with less expert children. It could be said that from these studies the children will get less thrill and less understanding than from the former approach.

However, others would say that in this method geographers are operating in the same way as scientists (and school geographers in the same way as research geographers) and consequently providing general statements which in this form of the study are objective not subjective assessments of the answer. These conclusions are comparable with the results obtained elsewhere from similar studies. The techniques used are firmly placed and are not studied for their own sake, as can happen in many less controlled pieces of work. Lastly the field work is structured towards a conclusion and is not represented by inert, factual information included just because it happens to occur in the area studied. It is also a method which thrives on so-called difficult areas and it concentrates interest on processes instead of on the actual land use of the country or towns.

There should, of course, be no conflict over these two approaches, as they have different objectives. In field work the objectives centre on the idea of teaching an 'eye for country' or landscape on the spot (Roberson and Long), while objectives in field research are based on the idea that all geographers should work in the same way and that children need to understand both the basic concepts of the subject and its structure before individual facts can be made relevant and intelligible. Considering these objectives it should be possible to decide where and when each approach should be used. Several observations are possible without attempting to go into detail on a field work/ field research syllabus.

1 Too little field research is being done in our schools today.

2 The use of either approach depends to some extent on the scale of the objective. If one wants to get a quick overview of, say, the Weald, a coach trip with suitable stops may be the answer. If, however, we want to know something about the relationship between rocks, urban growth and type of agricultural land use in the Weald, then field research is the only answer. A sample of points in the Weald and the collection of relevant data concerning these three factors could easily test some hypotheses concerning them.

Can these two approaches apparently so divergent be ordered into a whole? Perhaps they can if one accepts the idea that geography must adopt scientific procedures and methods, and must try to develop theory of its own. An extended and more generalized version of fig. 34 is seen in fig. 35. Here, in what Harvey calls a route to scientific explanation which is an alternative to the rigid Baconian one we all know, the solution to the dilemma posed earlier may be found.[5]

The first stages in his route, perceptual experiences and image of the real world, are a wider and more general way of describing what we earlier called field work. This is the place for the geographer to consider what he sees in the area, to be studied from his own restricted and biased vision or perception. This seeing can of course be the traditional viewpoint from a hill or vantage point, but it can also be seeing in the sense of gathering ideas from maps, diagrams, texts and all other types of media. Harvey, in *Explanation in Geography*, describes this stage:

> This information when transformed into some language, forms a mass of poorly ordered statements which we sometimes refer to as 'factual'. It is partly ordered by the use of words and symbols to describe it. Then by the process of definition, measurement and classification, we may place such partially ordered facts into groups and categories and therefore impose some degree of rational order upon the data. In the early stages of scientific developments such ordering and classification of data may be the main activity of science, and the classifications so developed may have a weak explanatory function.

This statement seems to describe exactly what went on when we did field work in the past. There is nothing wrong with this procedure, technique and objectives providing the study does not always stop at this level of scientific explanation as it almost always did. An obvious example of this level of study was the production of the land-use map which dominated field work in both urban and rural areas for so long. The production of the map was almost always the end in itself and from it only weak, explanatory statements were made concerning perhaps the relationship between rock and land use.

112

From this point in fig. 35 we pass into the process earlier described as field research. The image the geographer now possesses of the area he is studying will be intuitively structured by the development of *a priori* theory or models. This theory, new or new to geography or developed from earlier geographic theory, will allow hypotheses to be deduced from it which can be tested by the

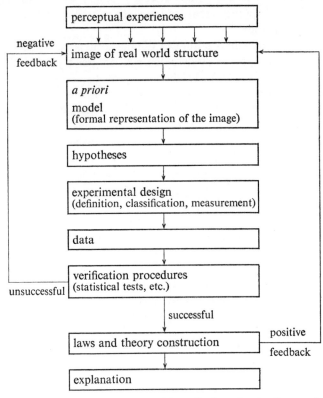

Fig 35. A route to scientific explanation (from Explanation in Geography *by David Harvey, Edward Arnold)*

geographer. In passing, it may be noted that hypothesis-testing that is not based on relevant and well-founded theory is wasteful of time, and valueless, as the results of the verification of these hypotheses are not relevant to the main body of geographic theory. From here on the procedure is the same as described earlier. At the end of the sequence the laws or theory developed will, if the verification has been successful, be confirmed with a certain degree of confidence and can be taken into the general theory of the subject to be used for further empirical testing or field research.

An example of this process can be described by an extension of the land-use study briefly described earlier. The student here has looked at the landscape and has perhaps made a land-use map of an area. He then develops an *a priori* model which could in this case be an adaption of the von Thunen model of land use around a central city. A hypothesis from this model could be that intensity of land use will alter as distance from the village increases. He then will collect the data needed for the testing of the hypothesis. Verification will be made, and the student at the end will have tested in the field a piece of theory developed originally from an east Prussian farm in the eighteenth century. A similar hypothesis that land use was related to underlying geology could be similarly tested.

This discussion has I think a number of implications for school geography. Firstly, that the two types of study in the field are really part of one process. Consequently, even when the teacher is trying to develop perceptual experiences of the environment, the child and the teacher must be aware of the stages omitted in the study and of the weak nature of the simplistic explanations made after this type of study. Secondly, the student must be allowed more and more to develop the field research stage of the process as he progresses up the school and grows in appreciation and ability. The observational stage, however, must not be neglected, as successful and rewarding field research can only come from a precise and intuitive series of observations about an area or a problem. Thirdly, it is quite obvious that field work and field research must be thought of as occurring in the classroom, the library, the record office, the parish chest, as well as in the more traditional rural and urban landscapes. Fourthly, it is quite obvious that if our subject is to be organized around a conceptual framework then the continuous testing of this theory in the field is essential, both for understanding and for the continuous development of new theory. Without field work or field research the theory could easily and quickly become dull, arid and deterministic; with it theory can become interesting, rewarding and probabilistic.

References

1 E. W. BRIAULT and D. W. SHAVE, *Geography In and Out of School*, Harrap, 1968.

2 G. E. HUTCHINGS, *Landscape Drawing,* Methuen, 1960.

3 S. W. WOOLDRIDGE and G. EAST, *The Spirit and Purpose of Geography*, Hutchinson, 1960.

4 I. L. M. LONG and B. S. ROBERSON, *Teaching Geography*, Heinemann, 1966.

5 D. HARVEY, *Explanation in Geography,* Arnold, 1969.

5 Assessment and examinations†

If we accept that one of the tasks of the innovating teacher is to be involved in evaluation, then this responsibility clearly includes consideration of the modes of assessment to be used within the evaluation. Many teachers would criticize the methods most often in use today as being too much concerned with the pupil's ability to recall facts and too rarely concerned with testing other skills of equal or greater importance. This criticism is sharpened when assessment is seen in relation to the growth of new approaches in geography and the emphasis on concepts. It seems best to define attainment, as others have done, in terms of a range of skills and abilities which pupils acquire, with the collection of factual content demoted in value but by no means removed from the scene.

But before assessment can begin, there is a basic need to define objectives clearly. It is interesting that practising teachers and educational researchers concerned with parallel situations in such other subjects as biology, history and chemistry have used B. Bloom's *Taxonomy of Educational Objectives* (see p. 159) as the basis classification for application to their problem.[1] This taxonomy has also been applied to the teaching of geography[2] and a series of example tests have been suggested, relating to each of the main objectives in turn.

The first of Bloom's categories, when arranged in order of increasing complexity, is *knowledge* and this involves the recall of information. Questions can test knowledge of specific facts, terminology, trends and sequences, or general principles. For example, many of the questions used when looking for the prospective company chairman to operate during the iron and steel game (see Part 1, Unit I) are essentially 'factual recall' in character. Slightly more complex is a question testing a trend or sequence ('movements of phenomena with respect to time', Bloom, p. 202), e.g. 'Describe the main improvements made in the production of steel from 1850 to 1900'.

The other five objectives, collectively termed 'intellectual abilities and skills', require the pupil to do more in the way of thinking and organising material.

Of these, *comprehension* is considered to represent the lowest level of understanding, asking the pupil to translate ideas from one form to another. This could simply mean converting a written description of an area into a sketch map – or, of course, the same process in reverse.

However, comprehension also involves the ability to interpret – for example, in explaining the changes in the coal and iron trade through the South

†G. H. Hones

115

Wales ports over the past 150 years, as illustrated by data showing the relevant exports and imports – as well as the ability to extrapolate, or extend a trend beyond the data given, giving supporting reasons.

The third objective, *application*, concerns the use of an abstraction in actual, specific cases. Again referring to the iron and steel game for an example its third stated aim is 'to relate (their) model decisions or hypotheses to the actual locations in South Wales, Scunthorpe, Sheffield etc.' Consequently a modern locational map of the iron and steel industry in one of these areas could be used as the basis for a question calling for suggested locations of the industry at previous stages in its development – thus applying knowledge learnt during the game.

Analysis is listed as the fourth main objective and this calls for a breaking down of information into constituent parts, the more clearly to see the relationships between these separate parts as well as their position in the situation as a whole. Selective extraction of data from a topographic map is regularly used in this respect to demonstrate a relationship that may well be lost in the detail of the complete map – between the patterns of settlement and communications, or parish shape and geology. Analytical studies of South Wales ordnance survey maps could well be practised, for example, to clarify the distribution patterns of coal mining, settlement, and steel works – in conjunction again with the iron and steel game.

The next objective, still in order of increasing complexity, is *synthesis* – defined by Bloom as 'the putting together of elements and parts so as to form a whole'. Data of the type collected through carefully structured field work exercises (see Vincent Tidswell, Part I, Unit XI) could be used in questions requiring presentation in map form, with subsequent explanatory description of the resultant overall picture – whether of urban spheres of influence in a region, or the distribution of glacial features (see C. Colthurst, Unit VII) – used to test hypotheses concerning their formation.

The last of the six objectives in the cognitive domain group (i.e. covering knowledge, abilities and skills) is *evaluation*. The relevant questions in this case call for judgments, qualitative and quantitative, in terms of internal evidence and external criteria – 'judgments about the value of material and methods for given purposes' (see Bloom). An example of such a question is given by Cox[3] as follows:

The pupils in a geography class have been assigned the task of mapping the land use in a small part of the rural urban fringe or a large city. The preliminary planning of the field work included discussion of the means of recording field observations on base maps. The following means were suggested:

a system of shading

writing notes on the field maps

a system of symbols

a numbering system

Appraise these four means and come to a conclusion about which one would enable the field work to be carried over most effectively.

This type of question readily lends itself to modification for use after working with many of the different teaching methods suggested earlier in this book.

Objective testing

At this stage it is interesting to note that Cox used a selection of objective questions in demonstrating how to prepare tests for use when applying Bloom's categories to the teaching of geography.

In testing 'knowledge' – requiring recall of such information previously taught as specific facts, terminology, or conventions – a number of straightforward question types are used.

One method is to call for the matching of items, as in this test of terminology.[4]

Match the definition with the appropriate name.
(1) the arch or crest of a fold in rock strata   (a) anticline
(2) the valley formed by the land sinking   (b) fault
      relatively between two roughly parallel   (c) graben
      faults/planes   (d) horst
(3) an elevated block bounded by two roughly   (e) joint
      parallel fault planes

                                                           etc.

Other very common types include the true/false question, or those requiring completion i.e. inserting the key words omitted from a paragraph.[5]

e.g. Immediately to the south of the...............in Canada is found the taiga or .... forest belt. Summer is .... in duration but becomes warm with average temperatures of the warmest month, namely, ..., rising to nearly 70° F. ....

Correct item selection from a multiple choice question is, nevertheless, probably the most valuable of the different types and can be used in a variety of situations. One example[6] is used by Cox to test knowledge of general principles as follows:

The relationship between temperature and altitude is that:
(1) as altitude increases, temperature increases
(2) as altitude increases, temperature remains constant
(3) as altitude increases, temperature decreases
(4) as altitude decreases, temperature remains constant
(5) as altitude decreases, temperature decreases

In another instance,[7] he tests knowledge of criteria with:

117

Shifting cultivation is a characteristic form of land use in many parts of the islands of Indonesia, because
(1) they are far removed from the main trade routes
(2) leaching causes rapid depletion of fertility in soils after clearing
(3) the people are migratory by habit
(4) the hot, wet climate causes the rapid regrowth of natural vegetation over cleared areas
(5) people of low standards of technology and culture are found in the interior rather than the coastal areas.

However, although their overall advantages in relation to impartiality, reliability, speed of marking and coverage of syllabus are broadly accepted, it is rarely appreciated that objective questions can be devised to test a variety of mental processes, and not just knowledge gained. Once this fact is understood and their disadvantages – for example, problems in construction or their inability to assess such subjective qualities as written style – are accepted as limitations and not barriers to their use, their value as a means of assessment complementary to essay-type questions will become more apparent. There are many occasions when geographers could profitably use them in a much wider context than hitherto.

In addition to testing 'knowledge', in written or graphic form, objective questions can also be used to test such things as the understanding of basic concepts involved (comprehension), or the pupil's ability to apply knowledge to other situations (application).

For example, objective questions could cover much of the subsequent testing necessary to see how well the aims had been achieved after a class had been playing the iron and steel game. A number of possible multiple-choice questions (as yet untested) are here given as examples, all requiring completion of a sentence by adding the correct answer to the first part or 'stem' as it is termed.

1 The most important influence on the siting of a new iron factory in 1820 was the location of
(a) the industrial area needing the iron
(b) the availability of skilled labour
(c) the major seaports
(d) the 'coal and iron' field
(e) the railway
2 The present availability of local low-grade iron ore is of major importance in the location of the steel works at
(a) Port Talbot
(b) Dagenham
(c) Scunthorpe
(d) Middlesbrough
(e) Sheffield
(Used with a map showing the places mentioned and major coalfields.)

3 A steel plant was built in Ebbw Vale primarily because of
(a) its nearness to the coast
(b) local supplies of iron ore
(c) demand for steel ingots by local industry
(d) industrial inertia
(e) governmental assistance to combat local unemployment.

Although this type of question could, in the main, be testing factual recall, one can reduce the chance of this happening by using questions concerned with examples not previously covered in the actual teaching situation.

Conceptual understanding could even be tested by asking the pupil to apply his understanding, learned through the game, to another hypothetical example, thus removing the possibility of facts being recalled.

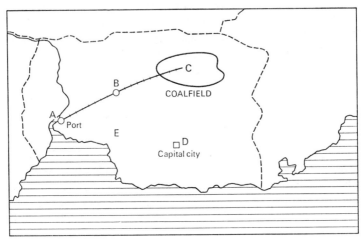

Fig 36. Map for Q 4: testing learning from the iron and steel game

4 The map represents a country with no domestic iron ore resources and no rail or waterway links with its neighbours. The best location for its first steelworks would be at

(a) A   (c) C   (e) E
(b) B   (d) D

In some such cases it may be preferable to use a graded marking scheme, rather than assuming there is only one correct answer with all other chosen completions assessed as wrong. In question 4, for example, two marks could be given for location A, one for B, and no marks for C, D, or E. Obviously this has the advantage of more flexibility, by 'weighting' the answers differently, but makes the marking less straightforward.

The construction of objective questions is certainly not an easy task and generally requires a great deal of practice and expert criticism before the items are complete. The next, very important, step is the pre-testing of the questions before they are used in an examination for which the results really matter. Not only must individual items which prove unacceptable be discarded but the balance of the whole test be examined.

This naturally presents many problems to the individual teacher and it is clearly preferable for a group, as in a teachers' centre, to combine at all stages – in item construction, pre-testing, and final accumulation of questions into an item bank. It is from such a bank that questions could then be drawn as needed, i.e. extracted for use according to the precise requirements of a teacher.

Although such a bank containing a collection of items indiscriminately selected would be of restricted value, one that was tailored to the planned requirements would be able to offer the correct distribution of relevant questions from a wide selection. This would still give considerable freedom of choice to the teacher building up the tests. It has already been suggested that this approach could be operated at a variety of levels in education, from local to national, for individual schools or examining boards.[8,9]

Projects

Another area of assessment in which the geographer is particularly interested concerns measuring the value of, and attainment in, projects, local studies or problem-solving exercises. The work involved may well have continued over a major part of the course, carefully related to the specific objectives as seen by the teacher, and thus provides a different opportunity in assessment. With the pupil given more room for manoeuvre within a framework, the teacher is able to gain more information to add to the profile of achievement, information not so likely to be seen in other aspects of the pupil's work.

What then are we hoping to achieve through such exercises? How best can we assess the results? Is it acceptable to grade a field-work exercise by overall impression, subjectively and without having decided upon the 'weighting' to be given to the parts, or the complementary objectives?

Can an accurate assessment of field work be based on instructions such as the following?

The candidate's field work should be marked by impression on a scale of 0–20 marks. Take special care to use as much of the scale as possible. The following are the qualities that should be looked for in assessing the candidate's work: accuracy of observation; clarity and precision in recording the observation by maps, photographs, models, drawings and in writings; accuracy of generalizations from these observations; correlations and explanations of observed facts – including use of reference material in arriving at explanations; touches of initiative and originality shown in the work; organization and presentation of the work as a whole. Look for excellences to reward rather than errors and omissions in penalize.[10]

Only if the six different qualities are given a specified weighting, and each graded separately, can even a structured assessment be really acceptable. Performance in each division could be assessed by awarding marks (out of a stated maximum in each case) or on a five-point scale, relative to a class average score of 3. Thus 5 is rated as well above average, 1 as well below average and scores of 2 or 4 as intermediate grades. Once the value of such a breakdown in assessment is accepted, it is certainly worth considering whether the gradings of the separate sections should then be added together to form one overall total, masking variations of performance within it. Similar problems of project assessment have exercised other subject specialists for some time and although rarely applicable directly, the results of their work are worth careful study.

A good example of such work has concerned the use of projects in Nuffield A-level biology and the resultant framework of assessment is given below. Performance in divisions I, III, IV, VI, and VII is assessed on a five-point scale and for II, V and VIII on a three-point scale by the teacher concerned. Only later is a total grade score compiled by the Moderation Committee.

Nuffield A-level biology project assessment
Operational Divisions – marked on a five-point scale except for those marked* (three-point).

    I Statement of problem
  *II Selection of topic for investigation
  III Investigation of background knowledge
  IV Planning of procedure
  *V Recording
  VI Inference from practical work
  VII Relating inferences to background knowledge: suggestions for further investigation
*VIII Bibliography and acknowledgments

A somewhat different approach is followed by a university department for projects in electrical engineering[11] where the suggested plan of assessment was stated as follows:

Project assessment
It is assumed that the purpose of a project is to assess a student's ability

(a) to understand a problem
(b) to conduct a satisfactory investigation into the problem
(c) to obtain sound results

(d) to assess, objectively, his own work and that of others

(e) to draw reasoned conclusions

(f) to communicate his ideas

In view of this it is suggested that the following sections could form the basis of a project assessment scheme.

	Suggested Mark
1 Assessment of problem and specification of its solution	10
2 Preparatory work – collection and analysis of information	20
3 Proposals for solution	10
4 Evaluation of proposals and decisions on optimum solution	20
5 Experimental implementation	70
6 Presentation of solution	70

   (i)   apparatus, graphs, readings, etc. i.e. record of (5)

  (ii) discussion to include statement on validity and reliability of methods and results.

(iii) conclusion.

In most such cases the fact that the teacher is involved in two ways, firstly as project supervisor and secondly as assessor, causes problems, If, however, it is felt that such work is sufficiently important for it to be included in the course and the assessment, then surely these problems must be faced. The best solution could well be a carefully weighted and structured scheme of assessment of the type suggested.

Structured assessment

To return to a broader view of assessment and the need for a carefully structured overall plan, it is important to see how a grid, or matrix, often used to portray a curriculum (see Everson, chapter 8), can also serve as a basic design for testing achievement – often termed a 'blueprint grid'. Based on the decided classification of objectives, such a grid provides a platform for the more rigorous assessment procedures which are long overdue.

The grid is constructed after making decisions on

(a) the subject matter (content) areas

(b) the objectives which the examination is setting out to measure.

In the example grid shown, the title 'Process' is given to a group of behaviours related to the objectives decided upon by the teacher, or team of teachers, concerned. These categories are based on a classification which is a simplification[12] of that developed by Bloom[13] and could naturally be modified in turn if wished.

Once the framework has been decided upon, it will be appreciated that not all the reference squares, or cells, will be used – some topics are simply relevant to specific objectives. For the remainder of cells, however, it is then necessary to enter in detailed requirements for guidance in preparing the actual questions.

Examination blueprint

	Process				
	A	**B**	**C**	**D**	**E**
Content topics	*Knowledge*	*Skill*	*Comprehension*	*Application*	*Inventiveness*
Agricultural systems					
.					
.					
.					
5. Dairying					
6. Market gardening	6A	6B	6C	6D	6E

For reasons of space and clarity, the example section chosen (Topic 6 Market Gardening) is now set out in partly expanded form below.

6A Knowledge: Define terms e.g. truck farming, intensive agriculture
Explain convention, e.g. 2nd Land Use Survey Key

6B Skill: Measure distance and area on a map
Extract map data selectively e.g. areal pattern of orchards
Construct histogram from statistics

6C Comprehension: Recognize importance of travelling time to market

6D Application: Apply zoning theory of land use to other area (using O.S. map as base)

6E Inventiveness: Not considered applicable

In this instance after the blueprint specifies what is to be examined, the questions (items) could be constructed for use with maps (O.S. and 2nd Land Use Survey extracts) and statistics, enabling various basic concepts to be examined.

It is also necessary at some stage to decide upon the numerical distribution pattern of questions (the variable weighting or emphasis given to different sections) because this will naturally tend to be uneven.

For example, the relative importance of objectives A to E and content topics 1 to 3 could be stated as follows:

Objective A 25% marks   Topic 1 20% marks
B 30%   2 20%
C 30%   3 60%
D 10%
E 5%

This could then be portrayed in another grid and the resultant range of emphasis applied to the main blueprint when deciding upon the number of questions for each section.

Objectives

Topic	A	B	C	D	E	Total
1	5	6	6	2	1	20
2	5	6	6	2	1	20
3	15	18	18	6	3	60
TOTAL	25	30	30	10	5	100

Examinations

Inevitably many of the issues discussed are also very relevant to any consideration of terminal examinations, whether internal or external. Although one might not accept that it is the terminal examination that largely determines the style of teaching, it is true to say that the examination is a major influence.

That this is now recognized by examining boards is apparent in a comment by the Joint Matriculation Board:

> ... it was customary in the past to regard syllabuses as 'examining syllabuses', not 'teaching syllabuses'. The syllabuses were to be no more than a framework on which the individual teacher could superimpose his own curriculum and his own methods of teaching. Syllabuses consequently were often brief and did little more than outline the factual material to be studied. They tended to encourage the construction of question papers giving unduly high rewards to factual knowledge and to lead to a situation in which many teachers and pupils directed too much of their attention to previous papers. At the same time the papers themselves tended to become stereotyped over the years.
>
> More recently it has become recognized that syllabuses and question papers, of whatever kind, inevitably exert a powerful influence on teaching and that, while it would be improper for an examining board to attempt in any way to define the objectives of a school course, it is the board's duty to define the abilities which each of its subject examinations is designed to test and, as far as may be practicable, the weightings which each of these abilities is to be given in the examination.[14]

Of course, the role of the examining board is such that the need for continuous careful consideration of an ever-changing situation is only too apparent. One of the many influences always to be borne in mind is that of current trends in the philosophy of the subject in question and the board has to act sensitively to changes in process. The GCE subject committees or panels, comprised of both practising school teachers and university representatives, have the responsibility of developing syllabuses which, while not reacting violently to every new idea, do nevertheless take into account changes in the subject, at either university or school level.

On occasions there is a clear opportunity, if not a need, for the examining boards to take a lead in such a situation and not just wait to be pressured into changes. A good example of this positive type of move was the new A-level syllabus proposed by the Oxford and Cambridge Schools Examination Board for 1969.

The reasons for the introduction of the new syllabus were summarized in an explanatory 'general preamble' as follows:

> Geography is a rapidly expanding and questing subject. At a high level new methods and techniques are being developed, tested and retained or discarded as appropriate. Inevitably the emphasis shifts from time to time. While we think it totally inappropriate that pupils at school should be forced to follow all the current fashions in geography, some reflection of the changing content of the subject must filter down to Advanced level pupils without upsetting the general stability of the subject. As it now stands the syllabus is not sufficiently flexible to allow this and accordingly the changes detailed are designed to let this happen.[15]

It was recognized that one paper in particular was controversial in style, but initially a wide choice of questions was planned, 'so that both those who wish to teach the older and proven techniques and those who wish to acquaint their pupils with the newer ones may do so.'[16] It must be noted that when the first papers actually appeared in 1969, the transition was effected by there being two sets, one for each syllabus, old and new.

In the new syllabus, Paper II comprises an innovatory section (A) on 'Geographical Techniques' and a second section (B), 'Systematic Human Geography', which is a 'modernization of the old Section C of Paper I',[17] styled simply 'Human Geography'. This modernization meant that questions in this section were to be based far more on the understanding of the basic processes in human geography and the ability to apply them to a series of topics. This part of the syllabus is set out in some detail in the new regulations as follows:

The processes will involve a consideration of:
(a) Location: geographical position, orientation, dispersal versus concentration.
(b) Scale: the ways in which size affects efficiency and production as for example in towns, farms, industries, countries.
(c) Transport: the 'friction' of distance, the media compared.
(d) Technological change: examples of the ways in which innovation has allowed a constant widening of human activity (an indirect way of assessing physical constraints).

The topics to which these processes can be applied are:

(a) Economic growth of nations and regions so as to evaluate the balance between physical and human factors.

(b) Population growth, migration and relative densities.

(c) Settlements: elementary central place theory, hierarchies of settlement, functions of settlements and their internal structure, degrees of urbanism.

(d) Industrial activity: types of industry, elementary location theory, reasons for concentration into industrial zones.

(e) Land-use: the physical factor in terms of resources, climate, fertility, etc. set against the human factor in terms of the market, demand, distance. Elementary agricultural location theory.

A few of the Human Geography questions set for the two syllabuses in 1969 are given below.

1969 I.C. *Human Geography* (old syllabus)

10 Examine with examples the ways in which the functions of towns may be reflected in their lay-outs.

11 What types of manufacturing industry are most closely linked to the location of raw materials?

12 Under what conditions do high densities of rural population occur?

13 What advantages and problems result from the increasing size of oil tankers?

1969 II B *Systematic Human Geography* (new syllabus)

9 What factors lie behind the spacing of market towns in an agricultural region?

10 How far do you agree that transport cost is the deciding factor in fuel exploitation and use?

12 Explain, with examples, why the location of some industries is said to be transport-oriented.

13 Justify the remark that the degree of clustering in a population pattern depends on the scale at which you look at it.

The syllabus for section A is even more detailed in specification and questions set (examples below) indicate the style followed. The awarders had previously stated that they were in absolute agreement with the sense of a meeting of schoolmasters in 1966, 'that the teaching of techniques must be related to the solution of geographical problems'[18] Questions were thus set involving the collection, representation, interpretation and use of information as follows:

1969 II A *Geographical Techniques*

1 You have to illustrate in map form the distribution of population in a British county. Discuss the possible methods you could use, the ones you would choose, and why.

3 What are the practical difficulties facing the use of (a) newspaper readership, and (b) commuter journeys, in an attempt to define the urban field of a large town?

5 In what ways can a morphological map usefully supplement a contoured map?

6 Comment on the shortcomings of using the average (the arithmetic mean) in generalizing climatic data and suggest useful refinements and alternatives.

Another major change was put into effect in Paper III. Instead of the previous 'conventional' arrangement for a Regional paper whereby questions were chosen for two regions, Western Europe and one other region selected from a group, the new paper consists of one section on the British Isles and another on 'Topics on the Regional Geography of the Rest of the World'. Questions are 'directed to a few major themes of central importance in understanding world-wide processes of regional change and development'[19] with candidates encouraged 'to include material from any continents they have themselves (sic) selected for more intensive study.' Among the themes of special emphasis suggested are 'Urbanization', 'Migration and Colonization', 'Resource Use and Conservation', and 'Regionalization'.

The reasoning for this change was set out by the Board in its introduction to the new syllabus as follows:

Paper III is primarily regional. We regard it as fundamental that a candidate should know his own country and be able to use the first-hand knowledge he has gained in the field – hence the section on the British Isles. On the other hand there are recurrent problems in geography and we see no particular merit in a candidate being able to discuss them in the context of one continent rather than another. As it stands now the Regional Geography, Paper II must almost inevitably include a number of questions which are interesting and stimulating and a number which are rather arid and answered by rote. We think our proposals should cut down the latter. Not that there is any desire to pass to superficiality. On the contrary the questions envisaged will demand a firm regional knowledge as a basis for argument – but as a basis for argument and not as an end in itself. The ultimate effect should be to stimulate regional geography in a proper sense.[20]

The rubric for the second section of Paper III (new syllabus) in 1969 stated that 'candidates are expected to illustrate their answers from regions they have studied' and the questions included:

8 With examples, examine why resources have sometimes been exploited without the proper regard for conservation.

12 Examine the importance of *either* railways, *or* airways in opening up new areas for settlement.

13 What are the main differences between cities in the developed and the underdeveloped parts of the world?

Naturally this type of syllabus change can have a great influence on the teaching of geography in school. For some teachers it provides a long awaited opportunity to introduce a new curriculum of their own design – for others it means the possible removal of a supporting framework of comforting rigidity. It is not easy for a board to provide the right type of syllabus balance in such cases but, as stated earlier, positive attempts must be made to do this.

Changes in the A-level syllabus, however, directly affect a relatively small proportion of the school population while a very much larger number of candidates are involved with any changes at Ordinary level.

Thus, when the Southern Universities' Joint Board, as well as restructuring its A-level syllabus, introduced major changes at O-level in 1970, the effect was more widespread. The previous pattern involved two papers – Paper I covering Principles of Geography (including map reading) and Paper II requiring study of the British Isles and one other region, selected from a group of eight. The new-style examination presented a shortened (forty-five minutes) paper entirely on map reading and a second paper of two and a quarter hours on 'The Principles of Geography', removing any specific regional emphasis or restriction of coverage. Free to consider whichever areas they chose, many teachers used the opportunity to introduce a completely new curriculum (see Sheila Jones, chapter 6).

It must be emphasized again, however, that such changes naturally create problems that require careful consideration by all concerned. While welcoming the freedom of the new situation, teachers still need clear information about the actual style of question paper being devised – and must provide, in turn, reasoned comments for the examiners. This feedback, clearly emphasized in cybernetic theory, is vital if the right type of external examination is to develop.

Methods of examining

In addition to this welcome evidence that some examining boards at least are modifying their syllabuses, there are also signs of change in approach to the actual methods employed in the examining. However, although some boards have introduced new styles of examination paper for other subjects, little as yet has been done for the geography teacher and candidate. One notable exception to this is the way in which some boards permit candidates to take their own atlases into the examination room – as long as they are on the official approved list.

A statement on 'Changes in Methods of Examining'[21] by the J.M.B. sets out its general policy as follows:

In the same way, it has been recognized that existing methods of testing need to be reviewed. Often a syllabus covers so much ground that a very wide range of questions has to be provided and candidates can opt out of parts of the syllabus in the examination. As a result, the examiners are faced with the problem of putting into an order of merit candidates who may have been assessed on what in effect are different examinations. Although the examiners may devise questions to test a wide range of skills the candidates, by exercising their right to make a choice, may in practice be able to satisfy the requirements of a question paper by selecting a narrow section of the whole field.

So long as the GCE examination continues to rely to such a large extent on essay-type questions, problems of the kind outlined above are inevitable. Objective questions, in which the candidate is provided with a number of possible answers from which he must select the correct one, make it possible for a relatively large number of questions to be answered in a single paper; this in turn allows the whole of the syllabus content to be sampled and ensures that all candidates answer the same set of questions and are judged by the same criteria. Objective questions are also valuable in that they greatly increase the reliability of the examination; since there can in each instance be only one acceptable answer, the marking of the scripts is a straightforward process and problems of examiner reliability do not arise. Essay-type questions are relatively easy to set and extremely difficult to mark. The reverse is true of objective questions which demand very great care in the preparation and selection of items, a large proportion of which have often to be discarded because pre-testing shows them to be unsuitable.

It is thus in line with these ideas that the board has stated its intention to produce a new-style examination for chemistry in 1971, and for other sciences in following years, with essay questions reduced in importance, taking up about one third of the whole paper.[22]

This same board, in its examination paper for engineering science (Advanced level), has for some years included not only (a) objective questions (multiple choice), (b) questions requiring brief (single phrase or sentence) answers and (c) questions needing essay-answers, but a fourth group in addition. This last type, of a style which should be of particular value in geography examining, requires the candidate to study given data, relevant to a particular situation, and deal with related questions. Statistics, maps and planning reports could provide the background material for a problem, and solutions are asked for. One major advantage of this type of question is the way in which it faces the candidate with a situation which is probably quite new to him and not one for which he has specifically been 'prepared'.

The Southern Universities' Joint Board is including just such a problem solving exercise as one of the modes of assessment for the new Alternative-Ordinary level 'Applied Geography' examination, commencing in 1973. After providing a syllabus within which a teacher has some operational choice, and specifying the abilities which it is intended to test, a variety of complementary methods of assessment is considered necessary to evaluate the different aims.

Certain CSE boards have also been revising their methods of examining. The Yorkshire Regional Examinations Board produced a new syllabus in 1969 'prepared specifically to encourage the development of abilities over and above the traditionally over-emphasized ability to recall facts', with the geography committee deciding what these abilities should be and how best to create a balanced examination.[23] It naturally follows that such rethinking concerning the clarification of aims and objectives, with related syllabus revision, has led to increasing dissatisfaction with the methods previously used in the examination. An analysis of an earlier examination by the Yorkshire Board confirmed 'the view already held by the panel that the examination (and probably the syllabus) have not so far encouraged the development of abilities other than the ability to recall facts'.[24]

Although it is clearly felt that the new examination should not swing to the other extreme and 'give too little weight to knowledge'[25], nevertheless, the trend is inevitably towards greater emphasis on other aspects of the situation – with the important proviso being to the effect that the change in examination style should not be too sudden.

Change, however, there must be. At a time when the external examination is under widespread general review, it is surely most opportune for geographers to consider their special needs – and make precise suggestions as to the changes required.

Must we, for example, accept that an examination has a time limit? Or can we reduce the additional pressures of the clock by allowing candidates to consider a problem within a generous time framework? Can problems be stated, and questions set, some time before the actual examination requires answers to be given?

Some, at least, of those involved in the development of the new geography must be prepared to look carefully at the problems of evaluation, assessment, and examinations. Changes in the style of the subject must be related to, not developed in isolation from, necessary changes in the other areas mentioned.

References

1 B. S. BLOOM, *Taxonomy of Educational Objectives, Handbooks I* and *II*, Longman, 1956.
2 D. S. BIDDLE, ed., *Readings in Geographical Education*, chs. 22 and 23, Whitcomb & Tombs, 1968.
3 B. COX, in BIDDLE, *op. cit.*, pp. 256–257.
4 *Ibid.*, p. 251.
5 *Ibid.*, p. 257.
6 *Ibid.*, p. 253.
7 *Ibid.*, p. 252.
8 R. WOOD and L. S. SKURNIK, *Item Banking*, N.F.E.R., 1969.

9 WOOD in A. W. BELL and D. H. WHEELER, eds., 'Examinations and Assessment'; Mathematics Teaching Pamphlet No. 14, Association of Teachers of Mathematics, 1968, pp. 34–44.

10 Secondary Schools Examination Council, 'The CSE: An Introduction to Some Techniques of Examining', *Examinations Bulletin* No. 3., 1964.

11 School of Electrical Engineering, Bath University.

12 WOOD in BELL and WHEELER, *op. cit.*, p. 19.

13 BLOOM, *op. cit.*

14 R. CHRISTOPHER, 'J.M.B./GCE: The. work of the Joint Matriculation Board', *O.P.* 29, October 1969, p. 18.

15 Oxford and Cambridge Schools Examination Board. New syllabus for Advanced level geography, 1969, p. 1/5.

16 *Ibid.,* p. 1/5.

17 *Ibid.,* p. 1/5.

18 *Ibid.,* p. 1/5.

19 *Ibid.,* p. 4/5.

20 *Ibid.,* p. 1/5.

21 CHRISTOPHER, *op. cit.*, p. 18

22 J. M.B. 'Examining in Advanced level science subjects of the GCE', *O.P.* 30, July 1970.

23 Yorkshire Regional Examinations Board. 'The Educational Objectives of Examinations with particular reference to Geography', CSE Research Report No. 5, 1968.

24 *Ibid.,* p. 6.

25 *Ibid.,* p. 7.

6 Practical problems

Much of the previous discussion would be stultified if it was found to be difficult or impossible to translate new ideas into classroom procedures. The teaching units in Part 1 of this book may help to show some of the practical applications of chapters 1 to 5 in Part 2. But there are many hidden reefs, ranging from pupil indifference to the existing examination system. In this chapter teachers explain some of the day-to-day problems which they have encountered and ways in which these have been solved in their own school situations.

The opening contribution from Peter Hore describes the sobering results of a year's research spent investigating how some of the new ideas were working in classrooms. He was able to observe the situation in a number of schools, with the co-operation of fellow-teachers.

A teacher looks at the new geography†

Teachers are not noted for their willing acceptance of new ideas. They are essentially practical and conservative people and need to be convinced that a new trend, idea or method has classroom application before giving it their approval. Furthermore they are suspicious of persons in ivory-towered universities and colleges of education, who throw out wonderful suggestions, without testing them in the white heat of a classroom composed, say, of thirty aggressive youths from a twilight urban area. It is not surprising, then, that the waves of innovation breaking over the subject are causing concern – particularly to those who have coasted along comfortably with Eskimos and Masai or the Midland Triangle and other regions of the world (assuming that they have heard the pounding surf of the new geography at all). Therefore, when the writer was given a chance to assess the impact of the new trends in geography on secondary schools, he felt obliged to try some of the material himself and to get other teachers to try as well. In this way a practical appraisal could be made of a range of new methods, and some light would be cast on the problems which might occur, in the place they matter most – the classroom.

The experiment was made up of eight lesson units most of which were more than sufficient for one thirty- to forty-minute period. They ranged in suitability from first to sixth form. The units themselves had a bias towards gaming techniques, partly because more of these were readily available and partly because of the predilections of the writer. In practice many of the units were used in several age groups, for example the iron and steel game (des-

†Peter Hore

132

cribed elsewhere in this book) was played in a modified form from second to sixth year. In all, seven schools tried out the units and some hundreds of children and a dozen teachers were involved. The schools were all in the Greater London area (except for one in Kent) and consisted of a boys' grammar school, a girls' grammar school, a Church of England mixed secondary school, a girls' comprehensive, a boys' comprehensive, a mixed comprehensive and a mixed secondary school. The populations of these varied from about 620 to about 1200. Children of all abilities were 'exposed' to the lessons and a few unstreamed classes were involved.

The lessons and the reactions
For the first year a railway building game was tried (Cole and Beynon, 1968) although it was used up to the fourth year in some schools. The game was very popular and teachers reported great interest and involvement. There was some suspicion that the game was enjoyed largely because of the competitive element and that educational spin-off was small. One encouraging aspect was that quite a few children who had difficulties in reading and writing coped with the game adequately and appeared, for once, to be on an equal footing with their more literate classmates.

The application of new maths to geography was tested in the first and second year by way of some elementary set theory. Based on Cole and Beynon again the unit looked at the spatial distribution and areal association of phenomena on simple maps. In schools where new maths was taught the children had no problems in tackling the exercises, although they weren't too convinced that they had much to do with geography. This attitude, oddly enough, was supported by the one teacher in the sample who had a degree in both maths and geography. Other teachers whose last experience of formal maths was some years ago, were highly suspicious of the whole unit. The impression was that a great deal of conditioning against new maths had already taken place. The subject had acquired a frightening mystique and the use of this monster in geography was too much for some. On balance teachers' attitudes to this unit were either hostile or at least negative. The writer was also made painfully aware that one class knew a good deal more about new maths than he did; they had to correct him on at least two occasions.

For those with a penchant for the new geography, the iron and steel location game is by now old hat, but for schools in the experiment it was new and exciting stuff. The version tried was based on FitzGerald's model of circa 1968 and with various modifications it was played by second-, fourth-, fifth- and sixth-year forms. The game threw up a number of interesting points, but above all it was enjoyed by everybody who used it. Some teachers considered that the geographical content of the game was small and that if anything it was more a historical-economic game. As a result in one school the head of history and economics expanded the game for use with the sixth form and has since become an avid gamer, producing historical, political and economic games of his own. There was widespread criticism that considering the time spent on the game (between two and four periods) not much was learned. There was also a feeling that a lot of rigmarole made very few points. In schools with numbers of remedial children there were difficulties because of the amount of writing needed. The board meetings necessary for the game exposed teachers to an entirely new situation. Many of them, including the writer, found it difficult to stop bossing the meetings. On the other hand, some English teachers who tried out the game let the children get on with it themselves, and all concerned found it very stimulating. It is possible that geographers are less comfortable with the creative, informal aspects of games than colleagues in other subjects to whom this type of situation is more normal. What was important about this particular game in two of the schools was that it revealed to teachers (and not only geographers) the potential of this technique. This was one of the most satisfactory results of the whole experiment.

Less successful than the iron and steel game was an island settlement game adapted from Cole and Smith (1967). It was felt that the competitive aspect was far too great. Most children, in this case third years, enjoyed the novel approach and played with enthusiasm. One class, on being asked what contributed to a group of settlers gaining control of the major part of the island, said first, the skill of the player and second, the luck of the random number draw (in this game starting points were based on sequences of numbers from a random table). The children did not think – and probably they were right – that things like mountains, marshland or rugged coastlines influenced the final pattern of settlement on the playing board. To be fair to Cole and Smith they would probably not claim that the game was perfect, but as it stood it was of marginal value in demonstrating how areas are settled.

Many of the criticisms voiced in the preceding paragraph can be applied to a farm operating game developed by Cole and Smith (1967), which was used more extensively than the island settlement game. Teachers thought that it depended too much on chance factors to have much value, even allowing for the recognition that chance is an element which has been ignored too long in geography. Like many of the lesson units, this game suffered from being played in a vacuum. If the game had been part of a syllabus dealing with agriculture it would have been quite useful in illustrating how one factor (climate) affects the farmer's choice of crops. Once again a fair amount of routine had to be endured, in this case writing down lists of crops for the sixteen fields for six years, to produce pretty small results. Nevertheless the children enjoyed the game, although they seemed very concerned with making more money at the end of six years than the others. This is, of course, an aspect of reality but even so teachers doubted whether the game as a whole enlightened children significantly as to the problems facing farmers.

A number of statistical exercises were constructed using geographical data. They were based on Spearman's rank correlation coefficient and were pitched at fifth-form level. Some were tried with the sixth. The pupils who attempted the exercises had few problems but criticized the lengthy arithmetical computations which were required. In one case they thought correlations of a non-quantitative nature could be made by simply examining the figures. They did not see much point in working out a figure, say ·2, which although precise merely put in numerical form a conclusion most had already arrived at. In three schools some statistics was taught to the upper forms and in two schools a few pupils took geography and statistics. These pupils tended to be scornful of the particular method used and in any case thought it was not a lot of use to geographers. The use of just one device does not result in a fair assessment of the potential of statistics in school geography. What the unit did show, however, was that teachers were extremely apprehensive about using statistics. Those who tried reported getting into tangles and having difficulty in understanding the instructions; their difficulties may, of course, have been due to the writer's inadequate and less than clear explanations of how to use the exercises. One must conclude, nevertheless, that at the moment geography teachers, at least in this sample, are ill-equipped to deal with statistical methods. An incidental point of interest is that mathematics departments in schools where these lessons were tried out, were intrigued by the gropings in their direction. For those geographers who feel it is a worthwhile line to pursue, co-operation with the mathematicians is going to be vital.

The concepts of time-distance and the 'elastic' function of maps were illustrated by an exercise taken from Everson and FitzGerald (1969). Time-distance rail routes were plotted between London and a number of towns and a distorted map of the British Isles was drawn up. Teachers and pupils found this a fascinating exercise and were absorbed by its implications. For many it was icing on the cake, an additional item to dangle in front of classes at the end of the summer term. What with the worry of exams in the fifth and sixth forms no regular place was seen for this exercise on the syllabus. This may be an ostrich-like attitude; on subsequent occasions the writer found the exercise relevant when dealing with London as a route centre, and this was as part of a traditional CSE syllabus.

Finally a unit on hypothetical models and land use was used with sixth forms. The ideas for this were from several sources but particularly Crisp (1969) and Everson and FitzGerald (1969). Unfortunately the unit was used in only two schools to any extent so conclusions are extremely tentative. The sixth formers who did the exercises found them stimulating. The unit gave one group an awareness of patterns in rural land use for the first time. There was considerable discussion about interpretations of the various maps and diagrams. Several teachers read through the information connected with this unit and thought it had possibilities, but most were sceptical of its value in the light of existing geography exam syllabuses.

Conclusions

There was nothing so startlingly different or difficult about the lesson units that any of them could not be used in the classroom. Similar advantages and disadvantages were noted in all the types of school and there was nothing to suggest that the lessons favoured particular groups of children. Further, the units for year three down seemed to be applicable across the ability ranges. Although teachers may have had difficulties in dealing with some of the material and with the situations created by the lessons, the children appeared to take them in their stride. There was undoubted resistance from many teachers to the units on sets and statistics, and many were not too happy with the free-wheeling atmosphere which can develop with the games. Quite clearly the games were popular and successful, at least judged in terms of interest and involvement on the part of the children. Caution must be exercised, however, in assessing their effectiveness as a device for learning. As has been pointed out, the amount learned was not commensurate with the time spent on the game, and the competitive aspect dominated too much. Even so, the games imperfect though they may have been, acted as an injection which stimulated new ideas among teachers in a few schools. The games may have lasting potential for the less able child, if only because of the improvement in motivation of a few difficult classes and children. If this is true it is an encouraging sign but a lot depends on the game itself. Kasperson (1968) in the USA, commenting on Metfab (Lansky and Stafford, 1967) the manufacturing unit of High School Geography Project (see Graves, 1968 and FitzGerald, 1969), found indications that the method was unsuitable for less able children The writer's impression after a year of using various games, with unstreamed classes is that they are one method of successfully involving in a common activity, children of very different abilities and aptitudes.

Of the dozen teachers who participated in the experiment only three considered that their attitudes to the subject had been positively changed. All teachers thought that some of the lessons had possibilities within their present arrangements, but few saw the wider implications the new methods might have for existing syllabuses, the regional concept and the very aims and objectives of geography teaching. One of the drawbacks to the experiment was that the lessons were isolated and did not fit into any existing patterns. For the sceptical teachers, the novelty of the lessons was, in some ways, their biggest fault. They were regarded as gimmicks, interesting in some cases, but generally irrelevant to geography teaching. Even those who found the new methods stimulating, who recognized its wider implications, were cautious. Huge problems were foreseen in redefining aims, recasting syllabuses, convincing other colleagues, finding the right public exams and so on. The first taste of new geography may be delicious, the whole meal could be indigestible.

In spite of scepticism and caution the majority of the teachers were intrigued by the experiment; only one said, 'I'll never make a new geographer.' It might be argued then that at least the right climate for change exists. Unfortunately, such optimism may have little foundation. As Gregory (1969a) suggested, although a large number of teachers were prepared to answer his question-naire (*Geography*, January 1969) and to co-operate in evaluating the changes on paper, this did not indicate real commitment.

We can conclude that in relation to new geography, a teacher problem exists at the moment. The children who took part in the experiment appeared to take things in their stride. In contrast many geography teachers are simply unhappy, particularly with the quantitative side of the subject. Much needs to be done by way of research, courses, books, articles, etc., to explain things to teachers and to translate the advances made in universities on the methodo-logical side into use for the schools. There is also a behavioural problem. Games show the teacher in a different light; the role of autocrat in the class-room dies hard and the amount of freedom necessary in, say, the railway pioneers game (Walford, 1970) is too much for some. This may partly be a function of the age gap – revealing the gap between those trained in the last five to seven years and the rest. It may be due to inherent conservatism. If so, new geographers will have a long hard fight to convince their colleagues that theirs is the way the subject must go.

References
The full account of the experiment referred to above can be read in an unpublished M.A. (Educ.) dissertation at the University of London, Senate House and Institute of Education Libraries, title 'Models and Quantitative Techniques in Geography - an Investigation into their Uses in Certain Secondary Schools', P. S. Hore, 1969.

John Bale outlines how three or four newer ideas were strung together to devise a fragment of a curriculum based on the new geography. As a result of his first trials, he concludes that a change in order and emphasis would be useful. Practical experi-ment such as this represents the mid-point between the introduction of isolated lessons into a course, and the restructuring of a whole geography syllabus.

A third-year curriculum fragment†

Part of a course involving some aspects of new geography

The description that follows outlines an attempt to structure four topics within the loose framework of a North America course. The main units were:

1 The railway pioneers game (from R. Walford's *Games in Geography*)
2 The boundary dispute simulation (based on R. Kasperson's provisional draft of material in the American High School Geography Project)
3 A 'compactness of country' exercise (based on an idea of J. P. Cole)
4 A 'centre of gravity' exercise to determine ideal locations for capital cities (also based on an idea of J. P. Cole).

†**John Bale**

137

The first two units took five thirty-five-minute lessons each, and the last two took two thirty-five-minute lessons each. In addition some time was spent with introductory and follow-up work. The class were a top-stream grammar school class aged thirteen to fourteen.

This work replaced a traditional course in the regional geography of North America. In such a course the above themes would have been excluded, and a list of places and products for memorization would have been put in their place. The belief in 'ideas before facts' therefore underlies this incorporation of newer material into a traditional framework.

Although external examinations were two years away from the class with which this work was undertaken the school had annual internal examinations. In later testing of the group, objective multiple-choice questions were used to examine their grasp of ideas contained in the work. The evaluation of the work is discussed in greater detail below.

Lesson description Unit 1

The settlement of North America in the railway age of the late nineteenth century provided the stimulus for the railway pioneers game, which aims to show that human decision-making as well as better known physical factors contributed to the location of rail routes. The children appeared to have no trouble in handling the concepts involved. Several independently reached the opinion that gaming could be an important contribution to such agencies as business and governments in helping them face problems. 'Official' follow-up work included the examination of actual rail-road patterns and a comparison with those produced in the game. (The game is fully described in Walford's book.)

Unit 2

The effect of the Canadian boundary on the USA was next introduced. It was noted that the border acts as a barrier to movement and that few railway lines cross it, while many run parallel on either side of it.

This led on to discussion of political boundaries and their nature. The boundary dispute simulation (now, in altered form, in the Political Geography Unit of the American High School Geography Project) aims at acquainting children with the following concepts: boundaries as limits of political territory; interruptions of the movements between places of people, goods, information and ideas; different reasons, used to justify political boundaries; settlement of most border disputes by a process of compromise. Skills in map-reading, evaluation of source materials and negotiation should also be developed.

For this game the teacher produces source materials which the children refer to in the course of their lessons. In brief, the game revolves around a boundary dispute between Canada and the USA concerning the Maine–Canada boundary. Canada wishes to claim land within the state of Maine, basing her argument on historical factors provided in the documents, and on the fact that a Canadian company is mining gold on the south side of the border. Other arguments are built up by a team representing the Canadian government using the documents provided. The teams are as follows: Canadian team (five members); USA team (five members); gold company (four members); international joint commission (two American, two Canadian citizens); arbitration committee (three members, none to be American or Canadian); Canadian and American citizens (made up of the remainder of the class). The teacher acts as the political moderator, though with a sufficiently strong personality a pupil could perform this role.

To play the game the teams study the documents, which contain material from which cases can be made by each team. Source material includes various acts stating the origin of the boundary, maps showing the location of the disputed area, imaginary interviews with disputed area inhabitants, statistical material documenting the linguistic/racial groups in the area, etc. From this material each interest group can prepare a case which is read by an elected spokesman before the international joint commission. The commission then reports, and while it is doing so the teacher steers the US and Canadian teams to close parts of the boundary, thus escalating the dispute. These strategic moves are presented at a press conference. At all stages other interested parties involved in the dispute – the private citizens for instance – have been able to approach their national representatives to put their point of view.

The next stage in the game involves a temporary change of scene. To illustrate the impact of the boundary dispute three situations are acted out, with the help of the drama department, each involving two members of the class. The first involves the owner of a motel on the Canadian side of the border. He is trying to convince the border guard to open the border so that his customers from the USA can enter Canada, and thus assist him in clearing his heavy mortgage. The guard is irritated after a tiring day. Another scene involves the same border guard in an argument with a Canadian travelling salesman who is in the USA on business but without enough money to stay for more than another day. His wife and two children cannot be contacted. Other such scenes, designed to show how the border closure affects the man in the street, can be easily invented by the teacher (or the children themselves). After such acted situations the compromise plan of the arbitration committee is presented and the dispute is settled. The ensuing discussion and follow-up work form a major part of the exercise; the feeling of the individuals in the impact scenes must be analysed, and the way the border dispute was finally settled, by compromise and negotiation, must be emphasized. The follow-up work can include a consideration of actual boundary disputes.

While children of thirteen to fourteen clearly enjoyed playing this game, certain problems arose which suggest that it may be better suited to older groups. The main problem centred round the children's inability to prepare water-tight cases from the documentary source material provided. In providing a mass of detail to be analysed in the preparation of various cases the teacher was taking a sledge hammer to crack a nut. With children of the thirteen to fourteen group, therefore, the source material should be relatively simple. At the same time the children must be made to realize the importance of preparing detailed cases to be heard by the commissions. Otherwise the lessons could be rather flat.

Unit 3

Decisions in political events such as border disputes are usually taken from the national capital. This introduced the next main topic – an exercise in national capital location. The children were first asked to suggest where they thought a capital city should ideally be in a 'model' country. The majority felt that a central location was the most suitable and they then undertook to test this model on real world examples. Each child chose a different country and found the location of the national capital and the country's centre of gravity. This can be found by cutting out the shape of the country in card and balancing it on a pencil point (the eventual point of balance is the 'mean centre') or by the method illustrated in fig. 37.

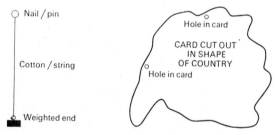

Place 'pin-end' of pendulum in one hole; where cotton cuts opposite edge of country mark in pencil. Join up point with this mark and repeat with other axis. Where the two lines cross is the area's centre of gravity or its mean centre.

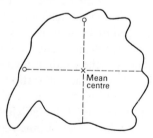

Fig 37. Finding a country's 'centre of gravity'

An attempt to test the models produced by the class was thus made. The distance of the capital from the mean centre of a number of countries was taken and the results shown in histogram from. The position of such places as Ottawa and Washington gave rise to considerable discussion. Conclusions regarding the locations of capital cities were written up and some explanations of location offered.

Unit 4

The boundaries which had been discussed in Unit 2 determine the shape of a country. The children were asked to think about how certain shapes, for example those of Chile or Norway, create problems for the countries concerned. The idea of compactness was introduced by suggesting that countries of quite different shapes might have the same area. The principal aim of this topic was to illustrate the idea of compactness, and to relate it to North American countries. In addition it introduced the class to the idea of ranking and of using simple mathematical techniques for precision. Again the children took a country each and worked out a compactness index, in the following way:

$$\text{compactness index} = \frac{\text{area of country}}{\text{area of smallest circle enclosing that country}} \times 100$$

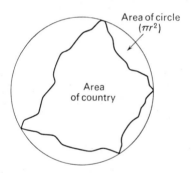

Fig 38. Working out a 'compactness index'

(Areas of countries can be found in most atlases; πr^2 produced the other calculation.)

When each compactness index had been found, the results were ranked from high (most compact countries) to low (least compact). Discussion then ensued about the implications of the findings. A most useful side effect in Units 3 and 4 was the opportunity the children had to discover a wide variety of places in the atlas – a new way of teaching 'capes and bays geography' perhaps, as part of a wider theme rather than as an end in itself.

Teacher's evaluation

Clearly the class with whom this work was undertaken enjoyed it more than conventional geography. There was also considerable enthusiasm which produced unsolicited projects on such topics as the East/West German boundary, and railways in North America.

As noted above, the border dispute game was, on reflection, unsuited to children of thirteen to fourteen, at least in the rather complex way in which it was presented. (The idea has been developed in a different context in the political geography unit of the final version of the American High School Geography Project.) It is also felt that another time, rather than to follow the sequence outlined above, it would be more logical to go from the border dispute to the compactness index exercise and then to the capital cities exercise.

No attempt was made to evaluate the work as a specific part of a North America course. The children concerned were not instructed that they were to 'do' North America. The exclusion of such an evaluation is deliberate since the object of such work is not a memorization of facts about North America but the grasp of concepts of universal applicability.

Many schools and teachers, however, may have to cope with aspects of the new geography within the framework of a traditional regional syllabus. Investment in the form of textbooks and equipment may not be easily written-off. The phasing-in of new ideas to the regional syllabus in the way described above may be one way to begin bringing realism, greater precision and more understanding of decision-making into the subject.

As the reorganization of education progresses, many schools become larger. The opportunities for teachers to lose their comparative isolation increase; a geography department can be a useful channel of communication for new ideas. Graham Stevens, teaching in a large London comprehensive school, explains how the iron and steel game (see Part 1, Unit I) was introduced to the rest of his department and how it made its impact on other colleagues.

Possible procedure for introducing new ideas in school†

The subject developments discussed in this book have coincided with the shift in secondary education towards bigger schools. Geography departments have become larger, as have the problems of communication, but there is a greater willingness on the part of teachers to try out new ideas. Like previous 'revolutions' (e.g. field work) the new geography is being introduced within, not in place of, the existing framework. Teachers find it difficult enough to keep up with the 'explosion of the data bank', let alone change the whole syllabus overnight. The following paragraphs are a simple explanation of how one new idea – the iron and steel game – was introduced at a large comprehensive school. The purpose is to encourage teachers to try out at least one of the ideas in this book.

1 Subject meeting
In larger schools a development in addition to staff-room conversations is the formal lunch-hour subject meeting to talk over, for example, the syllabus, the

†**Graham Stevens**

exams or the field-work programme. A written agenda and the limited time lead to effective discussion. The game was first introduced at such a meeting where its aims, and its emphasis on concepts rather than facts, were discussed.

2 Adaptation

The game needed adaptation for use in the school. It was decided to produce brief details of the technical background of the steel industry since the knowledge could not be assumed at the age of twelve-plus. The opportunity was taken to set a multiple-choice test on the information to reinforce important facts and to select the chairmen of the companies. It was also decided to have a 'right answer', although this was subjective and somewhat unreal, and to add the motivation of profits and losses in each round of the game. This type of adaptation process is vital to ensure the success of any new idea.

3 Discussion of classroom organization

In discussing how a class would actually play the game, problems like the materials required and the layout of furniture were discussed. The role of the teacher as 'recessive' (merely advising when asked, time-keeping and providing material) evolved. The most important adaptations, making the game suitable for all levels of ability, were decided on. The less able in fact formed only one company and the groups within the class took on the role of individual board members. This reduced the competitive element and simplified the game although profits and losses were still made, thus maintaining good motivation.

4 Follow-up

The game should fit naturally into the syllabus. Like field work, it should not be a treat or special event. In the concentric syllabus used at the school the game fitted in well with the topic 'heavy industry', following the study of coal-mining. It led on to a case-study of the Spencer Works, to south Wales and then to the industrial north-east of the United States. This particular game could be included in any regional study of a steel-producing area.

5 Duplication effort

The game requires about seven sheets of duplication and clearly there are advantages if this effort can be shared among the department. However, providing already duplicated material is a useful way of persuading colleagues to try out the idea. It is important to stress the trial aspect of the material and to involve everyone in its revision.

6 Other colleagues

The duplicated material was given to colleagues in other subjects. The science department was enthusiastic since steel manufacture was a topic in their second-year syllabus and it could be timed to coincide with the geographical study. The questions from colleagues, mainly about the utility of game-playing, were stimulating.

7 Public relations

It was decided to invite the headmaster to watch the game with one class. This encouraged a big effort to ensure that the idea worked. In fact the deputy head called in and managed to help one company lose £15,000. This is a good indication of the involvement new ideas generate.

8 Assessment

Subsequent meetings showed that the game was enjoyed by all classes and that the enthusiasm shown by pupils was reflected in improved exam results. The careful choice and adaptation of this first new idea and the interest it created has made other ideas easier to introduce.

The final two contributions in this section are from teachers (both in girls' schools) where experiment has had some time to develop. Sheila Jones, teaching for the Southern Universities' Joint Board geography syllabuses, has found it practicable to develop a whole new syllabus in which modern ideas are well represented. With the exclusion of regional geography papers at O-level from this board she may capitalize even further on these possibilities in the future. But, as she points out, whatever the situation in relation to examinations, the first three years of the secondary school represent a possible area of experiment, given some ideas and a resolve to try.

The assimilation of new ideas into a school syllabus†

One of the problems facing those who wish to use new teaching techniques, such as role-playing exercises, is that of integration into a traditional syllabus. It is essential that these methods are not used just for their own sake, but that they should form part of a planned scheme of work. In this way, pupils will accept the ideas as of value in their education and not presume them to be a teacher's gimmick for their entertainment in the occasional lesson.

After participation in a Madingley course in 1967 and discussions on curriculum in the Bristol School of Education, it was decided to revise the school's syllabus, starting in the autumn of 1968. In planning this syllabus, consideration was given to the fact that the terminal points in geographical education come at various stages, i.e. for approximately thirty per cent at the end of the fourth year, for another forty per cent at the end of the fifth year and for approximately fifteen per cent at the end of the A-level course. Planning was made easier by alterations to the Southern Universities' Joint Board O-level and A-level examinations beginning in the summer of 1970.

The aims of the new school syllabus were as follows:

(a) To formulate developing themes over a period of years in order to avoid the division of the subject into isolated and apparently unrelated pockets of knowledge.

(b) To develop an understanding of geographical concepts.

(c) To create an understanding of statistical information by the handling and interpretation of quantitative data.

(d) To encourage an increased awareness of the environment by
(i) direct observations and investigations
(ii) greater use of photographic interptetation sketches and map extracts, both British and foreign.

(e) To encourage, by the use of role-playing exercises, the development of critical and analytical thought, a feeling of involvement and an awareness of the need for planning.

Within this syllabus, briefly outlined in the table, individual members of staff have freedom of choice in their selection of topics, themes and techniques. Apart from atlases, few text-books are issued for regular use except in the senior school, and the policy is to build up a stock of book sets of varying types. The syllabus has now been operated for two years and although apparently working successfully, certain flaws have become apparent and there will be a re-evaluation of the scheme.

A notable feature of the syllabus is the ease with which it has been possible to integrate new techniques. Many exercises have been devised by a few successful innovators, but gradually more people are gaining sufficient confidence to develop lessons to suit their own requirements, and so the pool of available material is expanding. Most of the exercises used in this syllabus were obtained from outside sources and in this respect the school has been fortunate in having graduate students from the Bristol School of Education, who in their teaching-practice term have used techniques devised as a result of discussions with Dr G. M. Hickman in their method course.

Not all the exercises listed are used each year, nor is their location fixed. Already several have been used experimentally in different years (or with different abilities) with suitable modifications. Some have still to be tried. Although many of the quantitative exercises would probably be too difficult for pupils of limited mathematical ability, the role-playing games could be used to great advantage in mixed ability groups.

Two examples were devised within the department. The first was designed for the second-year course on agriculture, but could well be adapted for older pupils. The second was the conclusion to a term's course on urban studies in the sixth form. Neither was difficult to produce, but the Bristol simulation exercise was time-consuming. This is one of the major problems for those who wish to extend the use of such techniques. Even the simplest of role-playing exercises needs considerable time and thought. A second problem is evaluation, which cannot be successfully carried out until there is a wider diffusion of materials to all ages and abilities of students.

In conclusion, it should be stressed that those who wish to retain a regional framework can use these methods. The iron and steel location exercise has been successfully used as a theoretical model, modified to relate to development in South Wales and also to development in the Pittsburgh/Cleveland/Sparrows Point locations of the United States. It is the stimulation of critical thinking and the acquisition of an analytical approach which make these innovations so welcome. In a subject in which so much of the work in early years has traditionally been descriptive, these considerations appeal to many geographers.

STAGE	*SYLLABUS*	*KEY EXERCISES*
YEAR 1		
TERM 1	The acquisition of basic skills and concepts of scale, distance etc. OS large scale maps.	Selected exercises from and based on Cole and Beynon, *New Ways in Geography*, 1 and 2.
TERM 2	Study of Bristol and its region.	Exercise related to Bristol*, developed originally by Mrs G. Blight (Bristol School of Education, now of London).
TERM 3	Primitive peoples. How environment affects their way of life and how their mode of living is altered by contact with more civilized societies.	Eskimo settlement game, developed by Miss V. Caswall and Miss J. Fergusson (Bristol)
YEAR 2	*Agriculture* A study of the development and varying forms of organization of farming activities. Ranges from subsistence farming as in India, to wheat growing on prairies, to state farming in USSR etc.	Much use of case studies. Herefordshire farm game, V. Tidswell (Hereford)*† Von Thunen exercise based on Sydney.*
YEAR 3	*Resources, industry and towns* The various types of power and the development of certain industries. Urban development. Transport.	Iron and steel location, B. FitzGerald (London).* North Sea gas, R. Walford (London). * Urban field work.*† Railway building, R. Walford (London)*†

During these three years physical topics will be studied where appropriate.

| *YEARS 4 + 5* | Thematic/systematic work for both O-L, and non-O-L groups (fourth year only) Physical geography. Selected regional/case studies. Problems of food supply. Problems of power and industry. | Statistical exercises, e.g. on France (i) Air routes* (ii) Regional 'ordering'* Poverty game, D. Wilson and J. Brentley* (Bristol School of Education). |

		Practical problems
	Problems of urban environment etc. The local region	Weather forecasting simulation, G. Dinkele (Farnborough)*† Urban work.*†
YEARS 6 + 7	*Advanced level* See S.U.J.B. A–L syllabus *Urban work*	Field work. Bristol simulation exercise, S. Jones and D. Gowing. Population distribution, D. Gowing (Bristol)†
	Economic Transport	Network exercises and topological maps.
	Water	Linear programme exercise, Dr R. Chorley (Madingley, 1967).
	Comparative productions *Human settlement*	Use of log. graphs. Negro population in USA† Location of early villages† Everson and FitzGerald.
	Physical	Stream ordering, D. Weyman (University of Bristol). Field work on pebble lithology, glacial drift.
	VI special	Use of *Settlement Patterns*, Everson and FitzGerald.

* Suitable for older pupils.
† Suitable for younger pupils.

Margaret Caistor, working from a grammar school situation, outlines the modern approaches she has been able to introduce throughout a school geography course, while still teaching for relatively traditional examination syllabuses. She lists success and failures in considering the new material.

New developments in geography and their impact on schools†
Introduction of new developments into the curriculum

Within a three-year span a number of exercises and changes in syllabus have been introduced in geography in a three-stream entry girls' grammar school. The changes have ranged from the introduction of a specific exercise with one class to the re-planning of a whole year's syllabus, and they have oc- curred against the background of a regional syllabus; British Isles, Southern Continents, North America and Asia in the first three forms; British Isles and Europe for O-level GCE; North and South America for the A-level of the Oxford Local Examination Board. Geography is taught by two full-time geographers and two members of staff for part of their time.

In the first and second forms individual exercises have been introduced, including simple urban field work in the first form, an exercise on steel industry location in the second form and recently a role-playing game on the establishment of a new game park in East Africa was played as part of a joint biology-geography second form study of conservation in Africa. These

†Margaret Caistor

exercises have been introduced into the existing syllabus often by one member of staff at first, and then tried by other staff. There will be major reconstruction of the syllabus of the second form, partly because of the favourable reactions to the exercises tried, and partly in response to the success of the new syllabus for the third form.

This course has been reorganized so that although the area of reference is still North America and Asia, the work is arranged around topics and far more emphasis is placed on the understanding of ideas and concepts than on the learning of specific examples. So for example the topic 'water' includes work on river features, and on uses of water for power, irrigation, transport and multi-purpose schemes. Within each of these topics we have considered the concepts to be understood, the technical terms to be understood and learnt and the range of examples which can be used to illustrate the concepts. Wherever possible an element of choice has been included in the latter group, choice to enable staff or pupils to follow their particular interests and to enable full use to be made of the many different sources of examples available in school. A wide range of the new geography techniques is used in this course. Simple models are used of physical features such as land forms associated with rivers, and of economic phenomena such as types of agricultural organization. With close co-operation with the mathematics department simple quantitative work techniques are used and inter-disciplinary links are being forged with other subjects such as chemistry in the study of mining and industry and with biology in the work on agriculture. Games are also used at intervals; the iron and steel location game is used with follow-up work on the steel industry of north-east North America, and the railway pioneers game is used in the study of transport. The games used have facilitated the learning of the concepts concerned, they have given an opportunity for oral work and have engendered great enthusiasm; but perhaps most important they have provided situations in which each girl has had to use her reasoning ability to understand the position and consciously reach some definite conclusion in order to participate.

The fourth and fifth forms are concerned with preparation for O-level, all girls taking geography in the fourth form and about sixty doing so in the fifth form. There is considerable pressure because of lack of time and the syllabus followed is left to the individual teacher, although an outline syllabus on a systematic basis is available. This approach to the work allows for the introduction of new exercises as required and also facilitates co-ordination with work done in the third form. It is very noticeable that girls who have studied the new syllabus in the third form use the concepts and apply them in their O-level course, for example to the study of H.E.P. in Europe or to co-operative farming in Denmark. In map work use has been made of the Everson and FitzGerald exercises on the siting of villages and on the development of routes and the associated hierarchy of settlements. Both of these have proved very useful, they examine important ideas in map work, they can each be completed in a double period and homework, and they both have had noticeable effects on later work on the analysis of sites of settlements and on the location of routes as shown on Ordnance Survey maps.

One attempt at some new techniques with the fourth form was less successful. It involved a residential weekend which included as one of the topics studied a quantitative approach to an explanation of the varying growth of a group of commuter villages. The numbers of new houses were plotted and noted and correlations attempted with such factors as the distance from the railway station, from the main road and from sizeable shopping centres. Some correlations did emerge and discussion did result from the work, but it was not wholly satisfactory probably partly because it was not integrated into the general course, because too many of the ideas were new and perhaps also because it was too ambitious a project for the limited time available and the ability of the participating pupils. More successful have been simple quantitative field-work exercises with the fifth form in post-examination studies of industrial areas. These have included comparisons of suburban and central shopping centres and of varying pedestrian densities within each centre. In these cases the exercises have been an integral part of the whole study, the aims and ideas have been discussed and formulated first, the actual field work was straightforward and it has been possible to analyse the information on the same day. All these factors have aided the success of these particular exercises.

In the sixth form there are three main areas in which new developments in geography are being developed, the A-level course, the general studies course and the local studies course. The A-level course has been divided between two staff into physical and regional geography. In the past occasionally new topics have been looked at in the regional course but this year the syllabus was reorganized on a systematic basis. During the year the lower sixth will look at such topics as agriculture, mining, industry, transport, settlement and underdevelopment, covering aspects of each topic in South America and on a world scale. Obviously care was needed to ensure that the required A-level topics are covered and in planning the sections in detail use has been made of J. Everson's matrix idea. The work has included conceptual topics (it has been interesting that the girls accepted the idea of a model with no difficulty), descriptive work as in the more traditional approach and also exercises such as Tidswell's Herefordshire farm game and Gould's game theory exercise on Ghanaian agricultural patterns. For the section on settlement use was made of Everson and FitzGerald's *Settlement Patterns*. This new course has not been completely successful; some exercises will need modifying or replacing next year and there was initial resistance from the girls on meeting such a 'different' geography. This was particularly so from the girls entering the school in the sixth form. However, this initial resistance disappeared and as well as being a much more interesting course to teach there has been a noticeable improvement in the analytical quality of the work of the form. As well as this general

149

improvement in approach and analysis this organization has facilitated co-operation and co-ordination with other A-level subjects such as economics and economic history.

The local studies course has provided the opportunity of trying several new ideas in field work such as the delimitation of the central business district using a wide variety of factors, an examination of traffic flow and density, and a study of the hierarchy of shopping centres within our local urban area. These studies have been of varying success and although none have been a complete failure, the shorter topics which were completed in two or three weeks and from which meaningful and significant results were obtained have been particularly successful. The hierarchy of shopping centres is one such example, as it was possible to build on work done at the end of the fifth form, the surveying was straightforward but interesting, and a clear hierarchy could be seen. A lively discussion elaborated on factors affecting the hierarchy, and as the course is a joint one with economics the results were linked with a study of comparative prices in the shopping centres. In other topics, such as the work on the C.B.D. and that on the adjacency of types of commercial establishment, the results were less easily seen; they needed more time for analysis than was available and indeed in the latter case the area surveyed was too small for significant results to be obtained. However in these less successful cases the ideas have been met and used and far from being discouraged the girls are anxious to try out some of these ideas during their residential field course later in the year.

New geographical ideas have been introduced into the general studies courses of the sixth forms by geographers taking part in these courses. With one form, for example, a joint biology and geography study of water supply and pollution in Britain concluded with a role-playing exercise, 'Chayton Development'. Meanwhile with the other form a simulation game of the growth of a city from 1800 to 1950 was an optional exercise in a section of the course on the individual in society which culminated in the playing of 'Urbanization'. In both cases these games gave an opportunity for oral work and development of ideas and conflicts seen during the study of the topics.

Why have these new ideas been introduced into the syllabus? The first reason is that as our ideas of what we should teach in geography have been changing, from an emphasis on regional study to increased emphasis on concepts, so a change in means of working has been inevitable. The aims resources and method of working are closely interwoven in any course and many of these new developments are designed to develop the understanding of ideas and are very effective. Other factors of influence have been the desire to introduce more verbal work into a predominantly written course, and to introduce and use as wide a variety of learning situations as possible.

There have been difficulties and problems facing the introduction of new ideas, problems which have included the limitations of existing resources of textbooks and other material and pressures of external examinations. The problem of materials can be overcome only gradually, and external examinations, although they necessitate modifications, have not precluded the introduction of the new ideas. Perhaps the greatest problem is one of time, as any such changes in approach demand time for planning and discussion not merely by an individual but by all the teachers involved. However, given the willingness by staff to spend this time the benefits of such group planning are enormous. The interchange and development of ideas, the full use of all staff talents in preparing a course, and the general confidence and enthusiasm which such group participation engenders are all of benefit to the teachers. Meanwhile the girls also have gained from the changes. There has been a definite improvement in their understanding of geographical concepts and in their willingness to apply these concepts to any new problem or area to be studied. During the past twenty years the spread of television has meant that children have a wider knowledge of many parts of the world and the use of, for example, games or simulation exercises can enable them to use this background knowledge in making decisions about a situation. Rather than repeating static facts they are involved in a dynamic learning situation. In many of these new techniques there is a move to the pupil taking a more active part in learning. Decision-making involves individual task-identification and results in increased self-confidence through developing arguments and reaching conclusions. This increased confidence can be seen both in written and oral work. The new developments which are being introduced into the course have not all been perfect and have demanded time to prepare; but they are proving themselves to be enjoyable, intellectually stimulating and very effective techniques in the learning situations of the school.

7 Objectives

If individual ideas establish themselves by merit as a desirable part of classroom practice there usually follows a period in which the ideas influence the teacher's total scheme of work and objectives. Sometimes such influence is unconscious or implicit long before it reaches the stage of formal evaluation and consideration. Through such a process curriculum change often takes place. The satisfaction of new and interesting lessons is sufficient reward in the short-term, but it is possible for the longer-term implications to seep through. Such implications relate to the major tasks of redesigning syllabuses and developing co-ordinated schemes of work.

In this chapter and the next some of these longer-term implications are explored in the wake of Part 1 and the short-term issues described in the first half of Part 2. To some teachers this discussion may seem superfluous; to others it may seem tortuous or unfruitful. Nevertheless for many, one hopes, it may help to put individual ideas into a context. If new approaches to geography are to add up to more than just 'a box of tricks', discussions such as these will be needed to bring coherence and inner consistency.

The two papers on objectives which make up this chapter to some extent overlap, but this makes it possible to identify the two writers' perspectives more clearly.

David Gowing's paper urges teachers to take a fresh look at objectives and so to re-examine the purpose of much classroom work. His concern for the 'non-operational character' of many statements about geographical aims is balanced by an interest in curriculum theory, and particularly in the model suggested by J. F. Kerr in a significant book published in 1968.

Like G. H. Hones, he uses the well-known list of B. Bloom as a touchstone for geographers in assessing aims and objectives. His major questions are then taken up by Trevor Bennetts.

A fresh look at objectives†

'Our curricula are still geared to a society in which the majority would be engaged in manual work, knowledge once acquired had a permanent value, the age of puberty was seventeen, life was over at forty and father never bathed the baby.'[1] If one accepts this statement one must recognize the need to take a fresh look at our objectives and to re-examine the role and nature of geography in school. It is not difficult to identify the causes of increasing dissatisfaction. Pupils feel that present curricula have little relevance to their needs and so their level of motivation and understanding is low. Teachers are concerned that the raising of the school-leaving age and some forms of comprehensive reorganization may exacerbate these problems. New

†David Gowing

152

skills and new attitudes are required to meet the needs of a rapidly changing society. For variety of innovations in curricula geography specialists in secondary schools are looking to the primary schools and to the projects sponsored by the Schools Council, the Nuffield Foundation and the Association of American Geographers (H.S.G.P.). Above all they are looking to the changes in geography at university level.

The great danger is that new geography derives undue importance from our present dissatisfaction.

> It is characteristic of any reform movement in education that the persuasive innovators unintentionally set off the 'band-wagon' effect. To some extent this is happening. It is not necessarily to be deprecated, but it is clear that some schools and individuals acquire the reputation of being progressive and successful simply because of their association with prestigious projects or institutions, just as some innovators collect unjustified criticism from reactionary quarters.[2]

This observation is directed at curriculum renewal, but it highlights the central problem we face. Are we in sufficient control of the process of innovation in geography?

Gilbert (1961)[3] regarded new geography in the universities as an esoteric cult. This viewpoint would be more difficult to substantiate today, though the relationship of university geography to school work needs to be examined. There is an underlying assumption that the main objective of the new geography in schools is to provide the raw material required at undergraduate level. Recent changes in A-level examination syllabuses may seem to make a similar assumption. It is a fair criticism that this emphasis has been one of the failings of our educational system, in which the majority of our pupils part company with the academic world at sixteen.

> There are those who believe that many of our young people in schools should, after a basic apprenticeship to the craft and mysteries of geography, be applying their knowledge to questions which would be concerned more with the growth of personal qualities and a sense of national and international citizenship, rather than the continued pursuit of academic geography.[4]

Beyer and Dir (1969)[5] criticize the American High School Geography Project not only on these grounds but also because of the vagueness of its stated objectives. This is not to deny its merits, with which we are more familiar,[6, 7] but to realize its limitations.

A second assumption is that these innovations can be incorporated into the existing framework, because this is how it is taking place;[8] yet the teacher is not equipped to evaluate the relationship of the new with the old except in the most general subjective manner. New curricula may be required and here the teacher feels most vulnerable. How much children learn depends partly on his personal qualities and capacity to form good relationships with children and his competence as a subject specialist, but more on his ability to teach. This ability is often felt to be intuitive rather than a self-conscious systematic operation.

Curriculum theory concentrates our attention on the identification of objectives. Kerr's model[9] of the curriculum suggests that 'for the purposes of curriculum design and planning, it is imperative that the objectives should be

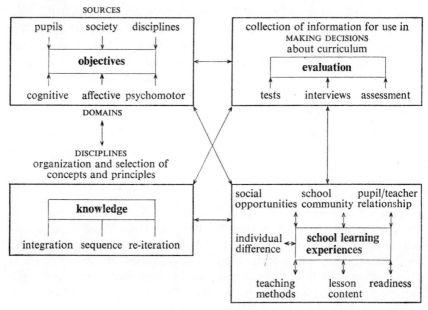

Fig 39. *A model for curriculum theory (from* Changing the curriculum *ed. J. F. Kerr, University of London Press)*

identified first, as we cannot, or should not decide "what" or "how" to teach in any situation until we know why we are doing it.' These objectives are the observable changes in pupil behaviour which are to be brought about and not the vague aspirations quoted below, which characterize the prefaces to many geography texts.

> Geography leads to an understanding of facts without a knowledge of which it is impossible to do our duty as a citizen of this very confusing and contradictory world. (Fairgrieve, 1926.)[10]
> It is important that they should have some understanding of the physical world and of human society in which they are growing up. (Newsom, 1966.)[11]
> To create a critical body of citizens who will not swallow whole the headlines of the press. (Marchant, 1968.)[12]

These traditional aims are perfectly valid but they are non-operational. They are the long-term outcomes of education and may be realized after the end of one's formal education, but they are subject to a whole series of environmental forces of which the school is but one. The gap between these aims and classroom practice is filled by more clearly defined objectives.

The most publicized attempt to identify these objectives has been the work of Bloom and his colleagues (1956–64). Their classification or taxonomy identifies three domains, the cognitive, the affective and the psychomotor of which the first two have been elaborated. Skilbeck[13] notes the danger of regarding the taxonomy as a source of objectives rather than as a tool to help in the systematic presentation and analysis of objectives.

Quite clearly there are different orders of learning here, each requiring a different set of teaching procedures. Bloom's taxonomy implies a psychological order of understanding and its application to geography needs to be more clearly marked.[14] See pages 157–9.

Cox's paper, in Biddle's *Reading in Geographic Education* is a most valuable recent contribution in this respect. Hirst [15] notes that a detailed taxonomy is a 'very good antidote to pursuing the usual limited range of objectives'; it deals with changes in behaviour that can be evaluated, though it does not make explicit their complex inter-relations. It is apparent that within the cognitive domain we have been content too long with the low order processes, the remembering of facts, the replicative and associative uses of knowledge. Ambrose, in his paper, is right to emphasize a shift in emphasis towards the high cognitive processes. But there is the danger that, in raising our sights, the applicative use of knowledge which is required to solve problems and to formulate and test hypotheses and which is more appropriate to university work, is being overemphasized in schools at the expense of the interpretative use of knowledge. This classification helps us to decide the facts, concepts, skills and methods most appropriate to our subject area and through which the objectives are to be realized. Such an analysis could lead to a further fragmentation of a subject on which widely divergent views are already held.

The aims implicit in the affective domain receive only lip service in geography.

To train citizens to think honestly, dispassionately and courageously for themselves about social and political circumstances in the world. Given easy access to accurate information and complete freedom to investigate, explore, debate and think through this data, it is likely important ideas, inferences, interpreations and conclusions will arise which encourage young folk to adopt co-operative, humanitarian attitudes of tolerance, impartiality and international goodwill. Political, social and economic exploitation or discrimination will be deplored. Prejudice, self-interest and special privilege will be shown to be anti-social.[16]

These aims are played down in school because they are difficult to evaluate and because they relate to what society often regards as private matters. Yet they are vital to the well-being of a society. The important values must be agreed on. This raises two questions. Firstly, whether the school should reflect or create social change; and secondly, how successful is it in modifying social behaviour. Musgrove[17] doubts whether the curriculum is very important in explaining social change. At present our work rarely demands attitudes, values and emotions. The real problems of pollution, traffic congestion, urban renewal, land-use competition and plural societies, people's problems often caused by the decisions of others, are not regarded as important and central to geography in school. The recent work of Cole and Walford in this country and the H.S.G.P. in America, point to the use of role-play and decision making as appropriate methods in this field. Even the syllabuses for the Certificates of Secondary Education constructed by teachers' panels have too often been shadows of O-level. Ambrose is right, 'It is difficult to be neutral about urban blight, ghettos or enormous speculative gains, nor should we attempt to be.' (See p. 80.)

Kerr's model of the curriculum inter-relates objectives, knowledge, learning experiences and evaluation. Having decided the objectives, the 'what' and 'how' have to be considered. It is, however, possible to take existing methods and content and see just how limited the attainable objectives are, and then to alter methods and content to widen the range of objectives. Curriculum objectives are above the disciplines or subjects which are the vehicles of the desired changes. This raises serious questions for geography about its place in the curriculum. At university, the skills, models and systems are the special applications of more general modes of enquiry. Are there skills which are unique to geography? The report of the working party on curriculum development in geography (Bristol, 1967) has this to say:

> Teachers are aware of the needs to formulate objectives which are in harmony with the emergence of new techniques and learning procedures at university level. Especially important at present is the application to geographical data techniques and modes of study being developed in mathematics, biology, community studies and the behavioural sciences . . . (However) . . . an unfortunate result of contemporary curriculum development, even in junior schools, has been to focus attention on individual disciplines without concern for their relationships to other fields and to neglect the overall structure of the whole school programme. We need to consider the types and relationships that should obtain both within and between the main areas of knowledge.[18]

The natural sciences, mathematics, the humanities and social sciences are major areas of knowledge which view the environment differently. Could our objectives be achieved more effectively if geography as a subject were abandoned in the curriculum?

The structuring and selection of the knowledge and learning experiences within geography again raise problems which have not been investigated sufficiently. Bruner[19] suggests that 'the teaching and learning of structure, rather than simply the mastery of facts and techniques, is at the centre of the classic problem of transfer'. A general idea or concept is learned which can be used as a model for recognizing other material as a special case of the idea mastered. The 'economy' and 'effective power' of the learning process are both increased through the use of structure. Hirst[20] points out that Bruner not only overemphasizes the cognitive domain in this concentration on structure, but is concerned only with a limited number of high-order objectives. Nevertheless, it is important for us to isolate the fundamental concepts of our subject and in this task close co-operation between teachers and university scholars is needed. (See the papers by Ambrose, Everson and Bennetts.)

It is important to decide whether there is a hierarchy of concepts within geography which should be presented in any special order or whether the 'foundations of any subject may be taught to anybody, at any age in some form.'[21] If there is no optimal sequence, then the growth of understanding and intellectual rigour comes from learning to use the concepts in progressively more complex forms. For example, the concept of location can be explored with infant children identifying their relative positions within a classroom or deciding where to place a hamster cage, so that all the factors which affect its best location can be discussed. Older junior school children, used to handling 25″ maps can locate their homes in relation to the school and services they use most frequently, the youth club, cinema, swimming baths, library and park. The child who lives the shortest total distance from all these points is at the best location, though the frequency of use and barriers such as main roads could be introduced into the measurement to show the effect of least-cost. In secondary school a network of routes and central places can be examined, in a matrix, to calculate the rank order of accessibility of each place within the system. The effect of constructing a new link road on their rank order reintroduces the concept that location is relative. The considerable effect of Piaget on Bruner's thinking is seen in the latter's analysis of the ways in which children think and learn.[22] Any concept or idea can be introduced, though the mode of representation will vary with a child's style of learning. In the teaching of geography much emphasis has been placed on visual images, the iconic mode of representation, but the new geography, with its interest in models, quantification and theory, would stress the higher order, symbolic mode. In practical terms, innovators must produce units of material, for any particular concept or body of knowledge, which provide alternative sequences of development, a wide variety of source materials and approaches to learning. Piaget has placed the child at the centre of educational process rather than the class or subject, but a great deal of research is still needed on the processes of intellectual development in relation to geography. Our understanding of how and when children acquire the concepts of scale, space and time needs a sounder theoretical base. It is this knowledge which will affect our specific objectives and the methods we use to attain them.

Examine closely what we teach. Why do we teach about Japan, volcanoes, glaciation, rubber, lapse rates, New Zealand dairy farms, the building of the M.5 or the morphology of the central business district? What does problem solving mean? What have been our conscious objectives? We have to look at the objectives of the whole curriculum, and at the specific skills, concepts and structures in geography which are important to us. We must relate these to the needs and abilities of the child before deciding on the methods which will be most effective in reaching these objectives.

References

1 F. MUSGROVE, *Contribution of Sociology to the Study of the Curriculum in Changing the Curriculum*, ed. J. F. KERR, Unibooks, 1968, p. 105.

2 J. F. KERR, Introduction to *Changing the Curriculum, op. cit.,* p. 7.

3 E. W. GILBERT, 'The Idea of the Region', *Geography*, Vol. 45 (i) 1961.

4 J. W. MORRIS, 'Geography in the Schools of Tomorrow', *Geography*, Vol. 51 (iv), 1966, p. 313.

5 B. V. BEYER and A. F. DIR, 'Implementing Curriculum Change in Geography', *Journal of Geography*, Vol. 67, October 1968.

6 N. HELBURN, 'The Educational Objectives of High School Geography', *Journal of Geography*, Vol. 67, May 1968.

7 B. P. FITZGERALD, 'The American High School Project and its Implications for Geography Teaching in Britain', *Geography*, Vol. 54 (i), 1968.

8 J. A. A. CRISP, 'New Approaches to Teaching Geography', *Geography*, Vol. 54 (i), 1969.

9 J. F. KERR, 'The Problem of Curriculum Reform', *op. cit.,* p. 21.

10 J. FAIRGRIEVE, *Geography in School*, University of London, 1926.

11 NEWSOM REPORT. 'Half our Future', H.M.S.O., 1966, p. 27.

12 E. C. MARCHANT, 'Some responsibilities of the teacher of geography', *Geography*, Vol. 53 (ii), 1968, p. 135.

13 M. SKILBECK, 'Curriculum Development, The Nature of the Task', unpublished paper from the Symposium on Curriculum Reform in Geography, Bristol Institute of Education, 1967.

14 D. SATTERLEY, 'Research Needs Underlying Curriculum Development in Geography', unpublished paper from the Symposium on Curriculum Reform in Geography, Bristol Institute of Education, 1967.

15 P. H. HIRST, 'The Contribution of Philosophy to the Study of Curriculum', KERR, *op. cit.,* p. 45.

16 N. V. SCARFE, 'The Objectives of Geographic Education', *Journal of Geography*, Vol. 67, January 1968.

17 F. MUSGROVE, in KERR, *op. cit.,* p. 108.

18 J. F. KERR, *op. cit.,* p. 27.

19 J. S. BRUNER, *The Process of Education*, Vintage Books, 1960, p. 12.
20 P. H. HIRST, in KERR, *op. cit.*, p. 60.
21 J. S. BRUNER, *op. cit.*, p. 12.
22 J. S. BRUNER, *Towards a theory of Instruction*, Norton, 1965, ch. 1.

BLOOM'S TAXONOMY
A Cognitive domain
Ordered on the basis of increasingly complex and abstract behaviours. They are both general educational objectives and a framework for those of specific subjects.

1 Knowledge   Emphasis on remembering.
1.10. K. of *Specifics* the recall of specific and isolable bits of information.
1.11. K. of *Terminology* of referents for specific verbal and non-verbal symbols. Definitions.
1.12. K. of *Specific facts* of dates, events, persons, places. Sources of information.
1.22. K. of *Trends and Sequences of* the processes, direction and movements of phenomena with respect to time of ways and means of dealing with specifics. Classifications.
1.24. K. *of Criteria* of the criteria by which facts, principles, techniques and procedures are employed in a particular subject.
1.32. K. of *Theories and Structures* of the body of principles and generalizations, together with their inter-relations which present a clear, rounded and systematic view of a complex phenomenom or field.

2 Intellectual skills and abilities   Remembering only one part of the complex process of relating and reorganizing.
2.00. *Comprehension*
2.10. Translation
2.20. Interpretation
2.30. Extrapolation

3.00. *Application*

4.00. *Analysis*
4.10. of elements
4.20. of relationships
4.30. of organisational relationships

5.00. *Synthesis*
5.10. Production of unique communication
5.20. Production of a plan or a proposed set of operations
5.30. Production of a set of abstract relations

6.00. *Evaluation*
6.1·. Judgment in terms of internal evidence
6.20. Judgment in terms of external criteria

B Affective domain
Attitudes, appreciation, emotional and social adjustment. Based on the concept of increasing internalization.
1.00. *Receiving* (attending)
1.10. Awareness
1.20. Willingness to receive
1.30. Controlled or selected attention

2.00. *Responding*
2.10. Acquiescence in responding
2.20. Willingness to respond
2.30. Satisfaction in response – involves positive emotional responses to stimuli

3.00. *Valuing*
3.10. Acceptance of a value
3.20. Preference for a value
3.30. Commitment. Conviction, loyalty, faith

4.00. *Organization*
4.10. Conceptualization of a value
4.20. Organization of a value system

5.00. *Characterization by a value or value complex*
5.10. Generalized set philosophy of life
5.20. Characterization

C Psychomotor domain   Types of muscle skills and co-ordination

---

Trevor Bennetts' paper covers some of the same territory as David Gowing's but in a slightly different way. Bennetts looks at the relationship of geography to general educational objectives and examines the type of imperfectly expressed 'general' statements so many teachers make when pressed to define their objectives. He reveals the confusion of thought that may lie behind apparently simple and innocuous statements. A close reading of his paper is a suitable preliminary to detailed consideration and development of any new set of objectives.

The nature of geographical objectives†

Geography teachers have an insatiable appetite for up-to-date information that will provide suitable content for lessons. Teaching methods are our stock in trade. But educational objectives – can we not take these for granted?

†Trevor Bennetts

The need for objectives, and their clear specification, arises from our concept of education. Peters[1] has described education in terms of 'initiation into worthwhile activities and modes of conduct'. We must ask, 'what is worth while?' The types of educational objectives that can be pursued are extremely varied, as Bloom's Taxonomy[2] has shown, and the selection of objectives and determination of priorities among them involve value judgments. The questions we must consider are not all of an ethical type, for some relate to our view of what is possible, and our decisions are therefore strongly influenced by our attitude towards developments in the relevant fields of inquiry – geography and educational theory. The arrival of new materials and new ideas can lead to new or more effective teaching methods. As geography and educational theory evolve, our views on what is possible can change. The review of objectives in education should be a continuous process, but the papers that have been given above make it abundantly clear why this is a particularly appropriate period for a reconsideration of our objectives in teaching geography in secondary schools. Aims, content and methods are inextricably intertwined but, as Hirst has pointed out in several papers, it is important not to confuse them. 'Adequate planning of a curriculum . . . demands first a set of clear objectives that constitute the point of the whole exercise, and then a programme of activities with an appropriate content as the means to the desired ends.'[3]

Statements of objectives have often appeared to be of limited value, either because they suggest idealism combined with unbounded optimism, or because they are so vague as to be unhelpful. What useful functions can we expect statements of objectives to serve? I would like to suggest two:

1 To indicate the direction in which we wish to move. This requires a general statement of aims that may provide a broad guideline or a necessary point of reference for future curriculum planning.

2 To provide a more specific guide that permits evaluation. This requires an operational statement of objectives, describing the changes in behaviour – in terms of knowledge, understanding, attitudes, skills etc. – that we expect as a result of the educational activities planned, and the description must be in sufficiently specific terms to enable us to evaluate our success in achieving these objectives.

Although it is convenient to identify at the start two broad categories of statements of objectives, defined in terms of their function, it is clear that the degree of precision required in a statement of objectives will vary over a wide range of purposes. In fact we may recognize levels of objectives, associated with distinct levels of educational organization or phases in decision making. Some levels in terms of organizational structure might be:

Organization	*Examples*
1 a school system	the secondary school system in a particular country
2 a part of the school system	the technical schools in that country
3 a particular school	a particular technical school

Organization	*Examples*
4 a course within the school involving several subjects	a foundation course occupying the first two years in the school
5 the contribution of one subject in that school	geography in that technical school
6 a course within that subject	a sixth form course on urban geography or a course on South America for less able second-year pupils
7 an individual learning episode	on the definition of central business districts or on a Pampas Farm.

Each requires a recognition of objectives, whether described in general terms for the school system or in specific terms for the lesson on a Pampas Farm. The need for educational objectives defined in behavioural terms arises when one has to plan an actual programme of activities. This is when consideration must be given to content and methods of teaching, and these should be selected in terms of their suitability for achieving the objectives. This point may be clearer if we look at an example. A series of objectives for thirteen-year-old pupils studying farming on the Pampas might read:

Given an adequate description of a farm on the Humid Pampas, students should be able to

1 draw a calendar of farm activities and relate this to a temperature and rainfall graph of the area
2 distinguish between fodder crops and cash crops
3 comment on the opportunities for farming offered by the physical environment of the Humid Pampas
4 comment on the following technological and farming developments that have enabled the Humid Pampas to become a major exporter of beef and grain: the railway system, the introduction of pedigree stock, barbed wire, agricultural machinery and refrigeration.

I am not here concerned whether these objectives are particularly worthwhile, but am trying to suggest how a fairly traditional set of objectives can be described in a useful manner.

Having specified the knowledge and skills that he wishes his students to acquire, the teacher is in a position to collect relevant material and select his strategy. Current practice in this country has been criticized, on the grounds that we use general statements where more specific ones are required, and that we fail to identify and describe general educational objectives where these are appropriate.

The objectives in one subject should not be isolated from those in others and should be seen in the context of more general objectives. It is possible to translate most general educational objectives into the languages of several school subjects and, at the other end of the scale, a single learning episode can be a vehicle for several objectives. Furthermore, the attainment of some objectives is dependent on the previous attainment of others. If we choose to think in terms of a hierarchy of objectives, we must recognize that it is an extremely complex one.

Fig. 40 is an attempt to show the relevance of statements of educational objectives to the task of designing a discipline-based curriculum. It outlines an idealized sequence which starts with the recognition of general objectives, and leads to the specification of objectives for a particular curriculum, the designing of that curriculum and its evaluation. The boxes contain information; the arrows indicate the movement of information; and the diamonds represent filters where the information is critically examined, and selected or rejected on the basis of some relevant criteria. The broken lines link the filters to the sources of information for the particular criteria involved. The discipline is shown as a source of objectives and as a medium for objectives derived from other sources. We will return to this later. The filters suggest three stages when clarity about objectives is essential if vital decisions are to be made on rational grounds.

1 *The Specification Stage* when general educational aims are translated into specific objectives for a subject curriculum. Although many factors can influence the choice of themes for a curriculum, it is important at this stage to ensure that the specific objectives selected are an efficient means of pursuing general educational (aims) and are appropriate to the discipline. The general educational aims and the discipline are thus basic sources of ideas for a subject curriculum and should also be used as checks on each other. The decisions made at this stage prepare the way for an outline plan of the curriculum.

2 *The Design Stage* when specific objectives are related to content and method in such a way as to produce behaviourally defined objectives. The discipline can usually provide an abundance of lesson content, and curriculum theory can sometimes provide guidance on the suitability of methods and order of learning, but, if curriculum planning is to be rational, the learning activities must be designed to obtain specifiable objectives. These can be defined in behavioural terms as decisions are made on content and types of learning activity.

3 *The Evaluation Stage* when the teacher attempts to discover how successful he has been in achieving these behaviourally defined objectives. The importance of this feedback should not be underestimated, although it should be recognized that there are desired changes in behaviour which cannot easily be measured, particularly those concerned with the attitude of the student. We need much more information on the likely lasting effects of the educational experiences we plan, but, even allowing for existing limitations, we could probably make much greater use of evaluation techniques. This has interesting implications for our examination system.

163

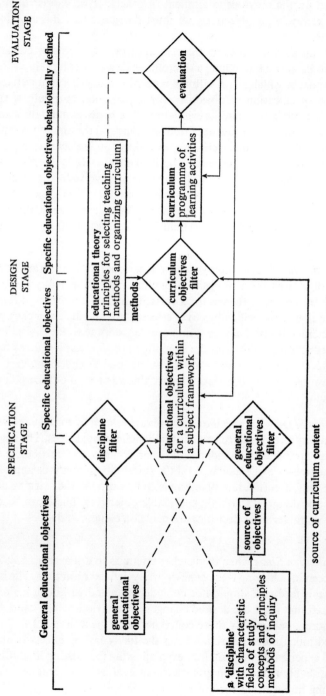

Fig 40. The function of statements of educational objectives in curriculum planning

It is perhaps worth repeating that the sequence portrayed in the diagram is an idealized one, and worth emphasizing that the programme of learning activities should always involve a measure of flexibility. Many factors, particularly the pupils' response, can justify a change in the curriculum programme. Evaluation is in some ways a continuous process, and this is all the more reason to be clear about one's educational objectives.

Fig. 41 is an attempt to classify the types of objectives that have been proposed at various times, by teachers in schools, training colleges and universities as appropriate for secondary-school geography. It is not a classification in a strict sense but rather an attempt to group statements in some meaningful way. Many statements of objectives are difficult to summarize because they are vague and open to various interpretations, and I cannot claim a high measure of objectivity in either the selection of phrases or their grouping. The diagram does, however, give some idea of the variety of objectives that have been suggested and it develops the idea of geography as a source of objectives and geography as a medium for more general educational aims. It also suggests many possible lines of inquiry.

Let us first consider the idea of a subject giving rise to educational objectives. A well-established academic subject is assumed to have a fairly distinct subject field, characteristic concepts and characteristic methods of inquiry. These combine to give the subject its structure. In so far as it deals with a particular area of knowledge and ways of understanding, a subject can be said to generate educational objectives. Thus the understanding of a particular group of concepts, or the ability to apply certain specified methods associated with a subject, may quite properly figure as objectives in a curriculum. Bruner[4] has claimed that the key to effective learning lies in understanding the fundamental structure of subjects, and this claim has appealed to many educationalists and has strongly influenced the major curriculum projects embarked upon in the USA[5] and UK since the early 1950s, most of which have been subject based. But geography has a very complex structure and this creates problems. Scarfe has gone so far as to state that:

> No subject can claim a place on the school curriculum unless it has a clear structure, a precise theme and a worthwhile purpose . . . if geography is to survive in school it, too, must be a scholarly discipline with a clearly defined purpose and a carefully organized structure. If geographers have not yet achieved this, the blame must be apportioned to geographers, particularly to research geographers, who, in recent years have added so much to the knowledge of the world that teachers in school have been hard put to it to know how to manage this unwieldly growth of content.[6]

This is, perhaps, somewhat unfair to research workers. The search for a 'precise theme' may be doomed from the start. Pattison[7] and Haggett[8] have both recently commented on different concepts of the field of geography held at different times in the subject's evolution, or even existing together. Haggett's

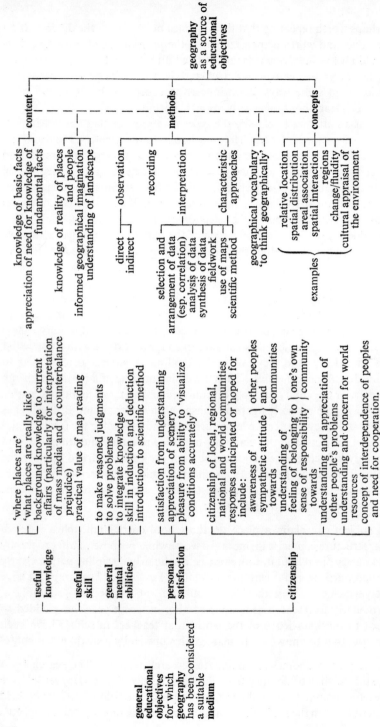

Fig 41. A classification of objectives that have been stated as appropriate for geography in secondary schools

use of Venn diagrams to describe 'the diversity of viewpoints within geography' does not suggest that geographers are likely to agree on a simple structure in the near future. We should perhaps be wary of over-simplified statements on 'the aims of geography' or 'the purpose of geography'. Ackerman[9] has suggested advantages in recognizing an over-riding problem in geography as an unobtainable goal to strive for, and Harvey[10] has suggested that viewpoints or themes act as directives, 'by indicating the sort of facts that the geographer ought to collect and by suggesting a mode of organization for these facts.' But he also points out that, because theory has not been well developed, it is 'difficult to identify with precision the point of view which characterizes geography and difficult to state the criteria of significance which that point of view defines.' A statement about 'the purpose of geography' is usually a statement of one point of view and, unfortunately, such views are sometimes narrow and give a tone of authority where no authority exists. In fact to talk of the purpose of geography is to conceal a value judgment. On the other hand, we can easily overburden ourselves, if we assume that we must give our students some comprehensive view of the subject, omitting no field of inquiry, and avoiding no major theme. In the secondary schools we are not training professional geographers, and it may be more productive to view our subject as a source of ideas, providing opportunities for worthwhile education, than as a structure that must be taught. But we must still face the task of selecting the concepts and methods of inquiry that we think will be most worth while, and here surely we must take account of recent developments in the subject. Searching for the structure of geography and reviewing present trends can clarify our views and reveal opportunities of which we have been unaware or which we had overlooked.

Geography as traditionally taught in many schools has been overloaded with 'facts', but short of useful concepts. The 'basic facts' do not select themselves and should be judged in terms of their usefulness. The criteria may be related to the concepts or methods of inquiry in which we are interested, or to objectives that, strictly speaking, have their source outside the subject – objectives like concern for world resources, preparation for citizenship of the local community and a background knowledge for current affairs. The confusion over 'basic facts' is well illustrated in a statement in the Geographical Association Memorandum submitted to the Central Advisory Council of Education in 1961[11]: 'All children should leave school with a basic factual knowledge of the world, countries, towns and people. The extent of this knowledge is a matter of some debate and must vary with different abilities, but it is commonly summarized as "sufficient knowledge to read the newspaper intelligently".' What precisely is the distinction between knowledge and facts? How can the requirement for some particular but unspecified knowledge be basic for all children and at the same time vary according to ability? What knowledge about which towns is required? What meaning should we attach to the phrase 'read . . . intelligently'? Not least in importance, which news-

167

paper shall provide our standard? The statement is not really very helpful.

The organizing concepts that have been most prominent in school geography have been the man-land concept and the regional concept, but the former has often been interpreted rather crudely, whilst we have used the regional framework as a convenient set of pigeon holes rather than examined its conceptual justification. Teachers are beginning to appreciate that the opportunity now exists to introduce more highly developed spatial and organizational concepts, and that students can be introduced more consciously to theory and probabilistic explanations. Bruner[12], the Madingley conferences[13] and the High School Geography Project[14] have made their impact, and many teachers are now not only aware of the developments taking place in the university geography departments but realize that these developments are relevant for schools. Although the stock of literature on the new trends, written or gathered together specifically for geography teachers, is still comparatively small, it has been recognized that the potential market ranges from the junior school to the sixth form.[15] The concern for more fundamental understanding has resulted in a greater interest in the analysis of patterns and the processes that produce the patterns, and some of the tools that have proved valuable to the research worker are also proving valuable to the teacher. The simulation exercise, for example, can make a serious contribution at both levels. The developments in geography in the universities are altering our views on what is possible and what we think should be aimed at in the schools.

Fig. 41 suggests several instances where an objective claimed to emanate from the subject is almost duplicated by, or at least strongly linked to, a general educational objective for which the subject is considered a suitable medium. This is as one would expect, and mainly arises:

1 Where a skill necessary for the study of geography is seen to have a wider practical application, as in the case of map reading – that boon to the discerning motorist planning his holiday route!
2 Where concepts are closely related, as with 'cultural appraisal of the environment' and 'concern for world resources', both requiring an understanding of the concept of a resource.
3 Where the practice of a method or technique is assumed to give rise to a more general cognitive ability that can be transferred to other situations.

The thought of general mental abilities may be very comforting for a teacher, but the idea has received little support from serious investigations. We cannot divorce the ability to solve problems from the form of knowledge involved or from the amount of knowledge required to see the problem for what it is. The geographical problem of describing and explaining the spatial development of racial ghettoes is fundamentally different from the ethical problem of personal behaviour towards racial minorities. The understanding of one may help the understanding of the other, but we merely fool ourselves if we believe that an ability to solve one implies an ability to solve the other. The scope for transfer is a matter of fundamental importance in education, but vague statements implying some general transfer effect do not help. We return therefore to the need for more specific statements of objectives.

The careful analysis of statements of objectives need not leave us disillusioned and impotent, and it can help us to think more clearly about what can be achieved and the implications this may have for teaching methods. We may first have to clear away some dead wood, but it should leave the subject in a healthier state. Let us look briefly at three commonly expressed general claims – that geography integrates, that it gives an introduction to scientific method and that it helps to prepare students for responsible citizenship.

The first claim is closely linked to the concepts of areal association and the region. Some geographers have been obsessed with the need to study 'total reality', and have seen the regional description as some sort of synthesis that enables to us comprehend a restricted area as an integrated whole. According to Hartshorne:

> geography . . . studies phenomena of unlimited variety in interrelationships of the greatest variety. This is not to be considered as a by-product of the nature of geography, or as a characteristic which, though common to all fields, is somewhat more marked in geography than in others. Rather it is fundamental to the very purpose of geography as the study of the reality of the earth surface, composed as that is of all kinds of things in all kinds of combinations.[16]

Furthermore, although Hartshorne appreciated that 'we cannot integrate the total complex', his only suggestion for easing the burden was that we should select features on the basis of their degree of interrelation and their significance to man. In the absence of any appropriate methodology it is hardly surprising that the quality of analysis and synthesis has not always been high. The conceptual breakthrough has come with the recognition of the importance of theoretical models and with the development of systems analysis. Faced with the complexity of reality, we need to isolate segments that interest us, to simplify in order to focus our attention on those features that we consider to be significant, and to structure our ideas in such a way as to emphasize relationships.[17] Models and systems are conceptual structures and should not be confused with the complex reality to which they relate, but their construction is an essential step towards understanding that reality. Our attempts at explanation have always involved processes of isolation, simplification and structuring, but we have not always been sufficiently aware of this. Geography teachers have therefore introduced models without fully recognizing that they are models and this has impeded rather than helped our students' understanding. If we are to capitalize fully on the potential of this valuable tool, we must place our emphasis on model building as a technique rather than on the model as an end product. This applies also to systems analysis. Although we may talk of 'real world' systems, it is more accurate and more useful to regard the system we study as interaction models with a particular structure designed to facilitate a particular sytle of analysis. In terms of structure, a system is considered to consist of a set of objects, together with the relationships between the objects and their attributes. A system which exchanges material with its environment is described as an open system and one that does not as a closed system. The concept of an open system is particularly attractive to geographers because it can be applied to the functional organization of space. System analysis is strongly problem orientated and the boundaries of a system and the set of objects and relationships are defined in terms of the inquiry. Systems analysis can be applied to a wood, a farm, a factory, a resource, a communications network, a city and any type of functional region.[18]

The second claim, that geography gives an introduction to scientific method, can be analysed in terms of what we mean by scientific method. Writers on school geography have not always been particularly explicit on this point, but it is clear that many link the idea to field work and the study of landscape – the 'landscape as the geographer's laboratory'. Emphasis is usually placed on careful observation and recording, and on the correlation of distribution patterns. Sometimes a strict sequence is also required, with instructions that 'gathering all the relevant information' must precede any attempt at explanation or theory. How we are to know what is relevant is not made clear, unless we resort to the rigid type of formula often associated with transects. We have great faith in the evidence of the senses and what Medawar[19] has described as the myth of innocent unbiased observation, we ignore the vital part played in scientific method by the formation of hypotheses and we are not interested in theory or prediction. The invention of hypotheses is too much like guessing, and guessing has been a dirty word with all sorts of nasty implications. Care in observation and recording are excellent qualities to develop, but we can add to them other techniques that are stimulating and provide a fuller picture of scientific method. Again, the implications for our teaching are considerable, both in presenting field work in a different light and in the realization that the scientific method need not be limited to the work in the field.[20]

The various objectives that I have linked together under the heading of citizenship, present very considerable problems, mainly because they are concerned with attitudes as much as with understanding, and we know very little about the type of teaching most likely to bring about adherence to value systems and forms of behaviour that we may strongly approve of. We certainly need to be clear about the types of attitude we wish to encourage and how geography can make a useful and proper contribution. The sense of belonging to a community and wishing to contribute to that community is one thing, but I presume that we would not wish to confuse that with narrow, exclusive attitudes such as resistance to all social change or rampant nationalism. What emphasis should be given to the local community, the home region, the nation or the world at large? Have we some responsibility to pay greater emphasis to the Commonwealth or the activities of the United Nations? Does this system of priorities extend to the Common Market countries or to the members of the North Atlantic Treaty Organisation? We are obviously on difficult grounds and in a vulnerable position. We should also beware of the assumption that cognitive learning will automatically affect behaviour as desired. This is one of the problems that has bedevilled social studies in the USA and the evidence we have is discouraging. Students appear to be influenced much more by their families and the society in which they live than by the attitudes favoured in the school. An inadequate course, particularly in the hands of a less than enthusiastic teacher, may do more harm than good. This is not to say that we should not be vitally concerned with attitudes, but that we must consider very carefully the contribution we can make. 'The understanding and appreciation of other people's problems' is an interesting example. Shave has stated that, 'Many of the world's fundamental problems – the growth and distribution of world population, the adequacy of food supplies, the significance and spread of disease, industrialization and standards of living, for example – are essentially geographical in character, and the geography teacher is in a unique position to help his pupils and the community.'[21] To describe these problems as 'essentially geographical' is, I suggest, to oversimplify matters and perhaps to misjudge the nature of the problems and the nature of geography. It is one of the traps of loose thinking about geography as an integrating subject. Geography certainly has an important contribution to make but history, economics, sociology and other branches of knowledge are also involved. It may be more useful to consider appropriate aspects of these themes as problems in applied geography, or to combine with other subject specialists in a team-teaching enterprise that considers the themes from various points of view. The second alternative has the attractive feature that it involves several teachers, who will, presumably, not only have their specialist knowledge but also different attitudes. The idea of a social studies course organized on a team-teaching basis, and additional to, rather than an alternative to, the specialist subjects, has much to recommend it. But I am straying from my theme.

The implication of the variety of types of objectives claimed, and the different priorities that could be given to them, is that we might expect many different types of curriculum, particularly in the early years of the secondary school before the external examination syllabus rears its head. Until recently one of the most depressing features of the development of the subject in the schools was the limited evidence of variety. Perhaps there is something in Musgrove's complaint:

Statements about objectives seem often to be little more than a rationalization of activities which are conducted for other, forgotten, or only half suspected purposes. They often have an air – in official reports, the writings of educationalists, and Speech Day orations – of a marginal commentary, an irrelevant accompaniment to an activity with its own determinism and private goals.[22]

If we are really concerned about some of the objectives that have been stated, our concern should be reflected in what and how we teach.

References

1 R. S. PETERS, 'Education as Initiation', an inaugural lecture delivered at the University of London Institute of Education, 9 December 1963.
Ethics and Education, Allen and Unwin, 1966.

2 B. S. BLOOM et al., *Taxonomy of Educational Objectives; Handbook I, The Cognitive Domain*, Longman, 1956.
D. R. KRATHWOHL, B. S. BLOOM and B. B. MASIA, *Taxonomy of Educational Objectives: Handbook II, The Affective Domain*, Longman, 1964.

3 P. H. HIRST, 'The Contribution of Philosophy to the Study of the Curriculum' in J. F. KERR, ed., *Changing the Curriculum*, U.L.P., 1968.
See also
'The Logic of the Curriculum', *Journal of Curriculum Studies*, Vol. 1 No. 2, May 1969; and
'The Curriculum', The Schools Council Working Paper No. 12, *The Educational Implications of Social and Economic Change*, 1967.

4 J. S. BRUNER, *The Process of Education*, Vintage, 1960.

5 J. I. GOODLAD, R. VON STOEPHASIOUS and M. F. KLEIN, *The Changing School Curriculum*.

6 N. V. SCARFE, 'Depth and Breadth in School Geography', *Journal of Geography*, Vol. LXIV No. 4, April 1965.

7 W. D. PATTISON, 'The Four Traditions of Geography', *Journal of Geography*, Vol. LXIII No. 5, May 1964.

8 P. HAGGETT, *Locational Analysis in Human Geography*, Arnold, 1965.

9 E. A. ACKERMAN, 'Where is a Research Frontier?, *Annals of the Association of American Geographers*, Vol. 53, No. 4, December 1963.

10 D. HARVEY, *Explanation in Geography*, Arnold, 1969.

11 GEOGRAPHICAL ASSOCIATION, 'Memorandum on Geography Teaching', *Geography*, Vol. XLVII Part 1, January 1962.

12 J. S. BRUNER, *op. cit.*

13 R. J. CHORLEY, and P. HAGGETT, *Frontiers in Geographical Teaching: the Madingley Lectures for 1963*, Methuen, 2nd edition, 1970.
R. J. CHORLEY and P. HAGGETT, *Models in Geography: the Second Madingley Lectures*, Methuen, 1967.

14 N. J. GRAVES, 'The High School Project of the Association of the American Geographers', *Geography*, Vol. 53, 1968.
B. P. FITZGERALD, 'The American High School Geography Project and its

Implications for Geography Teaching in Britain', *Geography*, Vol. 54, 1969.

N. HELBURN, 'The Educational Objectives of High School Geography', *Journal of Geography,* Vol. LXVII, 1968.

Six units of the one-year course, *Geography in an Urban Age,* have been published. The English distributors are Collier – Macmillan Ltd.

15 See, for example:

J. P. COLE and N. J. BEYNON, *New Ways in Geography,* Blackwell; a series planned for junior schools, and consisting of exercises designed to introduce young children to geographical methods and concepts. A guide for teachers is also available.

R. WALFORD, *Games in Geography,* Longman, 1969; the author gives much valuable advice on the use of games in geography teaching, and their construction, as well as describing six which he has constructed.

J. A. EVERSON and B. P. FITZGERALD, *Settlement Patterns,* Longman, 1969; the first of a series aiming at the introduction of important geographical concepts and new techniques of analysis to sixth-form students.

P. AMBROSE, *Analytical Human Geography,* Longman, 1969; a collection of significant papers by various authors with a valuable commentary by the editor.

R. U. COOKE and J. H. JOHNSON, *Trends in Geography,* Pergamon, 1969.

16 R. HARTSHORNE, *Perspective on the Nature of Geography,* John Murray, 1959.

17 R. J. CHORLEY, 'Geography and Analog Theory' *Annals of the Association, of American Geographers,* Vol. 54, 1964

P. HAGGETT, *Locational Analysis in Human Geography, op. cit.,* ch. 1.

R. J. CHORLEY and P. HAGGETT, *Models in Geography, op. cit.,* ch 1, 'Models, Paradigms and the New Geography'.

18 A Penguin paperback, *Systems thinking,* ed. F. E. EMERY, although orientated towards management studies, contains a number of papers that provide a useful introduction to systems' concepts, notably:

L. VON BRETALANFFY, 'The Theory of open systems in Physics and Biology', 1950.

D. KATZ and R. L. KAHN, 'Common characteristics of open systems', 1966.

R. L. ACKOFF, 'Systems, Organization and Interdisciplinary Research', 1960.

Within geographical literature the following either discuss systems theory or adopt a systems approach:

B. J. L. BERRY, 'Cities as Systems within Systems of Cities' in *Regional Development and Planning,* ed. J. FRIEDMANN and W. ALONSO, 1964.

D. R. STODDART, 'Geography and the Ecological Approach: the Ecosystem as a Geographical Principle and Method', *Geography,* Vol. 50, 1965.

P. HAGGETT, *op. cit.*

D. HARVEY, *Explanation in Geography,* ch 23, 'Systems'.

T. J. WILBANKS and R. SYMANSKI, 'What is Systems Analysis', *Professional Geographer,* Vol. 20 No. 2, March 1968.

D. C. FOOTE and B. GREER-WOOTTEN, 'An approach to Systems Analysis in Cultural Geography', *Professional Geographer,* Vol. 20 No. 2, March 1968.

R. MCDANIEL and M. E. ELIOT HIRST, 'A Systems Analytical Approach to Economic Geography', *Commission on College Geography, Publication No. 8,* Association of American Geographers, 1968.

C. M. HARRISON, 'The Ecosystem and the Community in Biogeography'.

D. R. HARRIS, 'The Ecology of Agricultural Systems'.

G. MANNERS, 'New Resource Evaluations'.

The last three papers are all contained in *Trends in Geography,* ed. R. U. COOKE and J. H. JOHNSON.

19 P. B. MEDAWAR, *Induction and Intuition in Scientific Thought.*

20 See elsewhere in this volume:

B. FITZGERALD, 'The Need for a Scientific Approach in Geography'.

J. A. EVERSON, 'Field work in School Geography'.

W. V. TIDSWELL, 'Towards a Structured Investigation of Environment'.

21 D. SHAVE, 'The Secondary Modern School' in M. LONG, General Editor, *Handbook for Geography Teachers,* Methuen, 5th edition, 1964 .

22 F. MUSGROVE, 'Curriculum Objectives', *Journal of Curriculum Studies,* Vol. 1 No. 1, November 1968.

8 The curriculum

This final chapter takes the discussion of objectives into the realms of practical implementation; their ultimate effect will reveal itself consciously or unconsciously in the curriculum that a school adopts.

Rex Beddis, in the first contribution, is concerned with the content of what we should teach. He takes into account such factors as the practical constraints of classroom and examination, available resources and 'what the children are interested in', but argues that these should never determine the curriculum. He urges a greater commitment to a subject-based curriculum, grounded firmly on key ideas in the discipline of geography and he echoes the position of Peter Ambrose in the first chapter of Part 2.

Developing the curriculum – a reconsideration of content†

There have been a number of significant changes in the teaching of geography over the past two decades. Amongst the earlier of these was the emphasis on realism, with the use of audio-visual aids, case studies and direct observation in the field. The method was essentially inductive learning from the observed and measured data. More recently, there has been increasing interest in deductive ways of thinking, hypothesis testing, precision in description and analysis and the use of simulation and games techniques. Throughout the period there has been a growing concern for pupil involvement, and a realization that understanding is more important than mere rote learning.

While there has been some changes in subject matter, as seen in the development of urban themes, greatest change has been in teaching method. We still tend to use the range of stimulating techniques and resources mentioned above to teach conventional subject matter in a traditional curriculum structure.

Many teachers have for a long time been unhappy about the rapidly increasing body of facts they felt obliged to teach, the sterile and unstimulating nature of the learning asked of pupils, and the naïve and trivial explaining involved. During this time developments in the subject at university level and in educational theory have reinforced this dissatisfaction, but they have also pointed to a way out of our difficulties. As suggested above, the greatest impact so far has been on the quality of individual lessons. What is needed is a rethinking of the content or subject matter that we wish to teach, and of the sequence in which this subject content might be most effectively introduced.

†**Rex Beddis**

The first task is to determine a worthwhile content for our geography courses. What is worthwhile depends on what we hope to achieve, and this theme of objectives has been treated earlier. The total content cannot be taught instantaneously, of course, and in the conventional situation it is split into lesson units spread over a number of years. The second problem, then, is to establish suitable content for these individual lessons and to devise effective sequence in which the lesson content might be introduced. This paper discusses the principles that should guide us in choosing the content of a course.

Objectives in geography teaching. Ideals and realities
All educational resources, and that includes teachers, are for the benefit of the pupils, and all educational activities should be designed to produce desired change in the pupils. There may be vigorous debate about what this change should be. Different societies will aim for different objectives, and it is fairly certain that the objectives of Chinese education are different from those of the United States. Within a country such as ours objectives may vary from school to school. It is likely that a comprehensive school is working towards objectives rather different from those of a highly selective grammar school, or in a different sphere, of a socially selective independent school. What is the role of the subject teacher in this situation? It is logical to presume that he or she is being asked to use the particular qualities of the subject to contribute to the general objectives of the school as effectively as possible. The geography teacher is being asked to work towards certain objectives (even if these are usually inarticulately expressed) as part of a team of teachers in the school. The geography (or any specialist) teacher should seek to use the subject to achieve these objectives, and as such there may be areas in which he is relatively ineffective. It is the responsibility of the headmaster to ensure that all objectives are being worked for, not the responsibility of the individual specialist teacher. The geography teacher has been particularly prone to the seduction of teaching anything that no one else wants to touch. Perhaps it flatters us to have the image of the 'widely educated man'. But it is an unwise role to play. We could be more effective, perhaps, if we concentrated on our particular contribution. (There is debate, of course, as to the value of subject teaching at all. This is another issue, and all that need be said here is that this whole volume implies a belief in the positive value of subject-based work in secondary schools.) The problem is, what content and methodology can geography offer as a contribution towards reaching these broad specified objectives?

We must realize that there are a number of constraints that will restrict what we might like to teach. They are fairly obvious. There are those that fall in the broad category of 'the teaching context'. A simple example is the constraint of time. Other things being equal, we are less effective with fewer lessons than we are with more lessons. Yet we must accept that we are only part of a team, and our lesson time must be restricted by external demands.

Again, other things being equal, we are likely to be more effective if we have a wealth of aids such as film strips, overhead projectors and laboratory assistants than if we have not got them. The significant point is that these are also the result of external influences – the availability of money.

Another example of controls external to our choice is that of time-table structure. We might need a long session, perhaps out of doors, for the effective teaching of some theme or method. If a headmaster insists on forty-minute lessons within the confines of the classroom we shall be hindered in our task. It is as though we say to the headmaster, 'I could contribute to achieving certain objectives with these pupils by teaching geography, but because of these external constraints my contribution will be smaller than it might have been.' In this sense, and unless we want to suffer a nervous breakdown, we restrict our objectives and modify our curriculum content and structure. The only alternative is to persuade the headmaster, or other authority, of the value of one's contribution, and so get the constraints removed. But, as all teachers know, this is extremely difficult.

Principles guiding the choice of content for a school geography course
The red-herrings, seducers and sources of confusion
We have always had some guiding principles (although often difficult to perceive in the anarchy of the English situation) in choosing curriculum subject matter. The following seem to be false and inadequate. It is not suggested that they are unimportant and unworthy of consideration. It is claimed rather that the content of a geography course should not be determined by them. The content of our courses often is, but never should be, determined by:

1 *What the current examinations will test* If examiners and teachers agreed fully on objectives, content and methods, there would be no problem here. A valid curriculum would be established, and examiners employed to test what had been done. What happens is often the exact opposite. Teachers, aware of their obligation to pupils, assiduously study past papers in the hope of predicting what might be examined. They certainly are influenced by the syllabus. Moreover this domination extends down into the younger classes and even into those where the examination will not even be sat. This would be acceptable if the examinations were in tune with the latest developments in the subject. But with few exceptions they tend to lag a long way behind such developments. One can understand, to a certain extent, the need for the examiner to serve the needs of the more conservative teachers, but if this is taken too far worthwhile innovation will be unnecessarily delayed. Teachers are reluctant to spend time on any theme or method if it is not going to contribute to the success of their pupils in examinations. Surely, though, a compromise can be reached to allow both stability and innovation. Mode 3 of the CSE examination, teacher-run examinations and discussion between teachers and examiners that produce syllabuses such as the new alternative Oxford and Cambridge A-level, show what is possible. But even in these enlightened situations the examinations must follow, not determine, content.

What happens if the influential examiner is positively hostile to change is another, sadder, situation.

2 *What pupils are interested in* It would be foolish to ignore the interests of pupils in considering the content or teaching method of a lesson, but this is a far cry from suggesting that the limited, half-understood and inconsistent interests of adolescents should actually determine the content of a course. We have an obligation to develop interests, to engender new ones as yet unknown to our pupils, to stimulate and provoke. It is obvious that we should look elsewhere for some guide as to what aspects of geography to teach.

3 *What resources are available* Most teachers must have scrapped their plans for a lesson because an unexpected and valuable aid or resource has become available. A film arrives at the school for a week, and although it does not fit readily in the course at this point, we are tempted into using it because of its high quality. Or we find an occasion near the end of term where we may do work out of doors, so our programme is switched to allow for field work. Only a pedant would suggest that this could be disastrous. What would be wrong, however, would be to introduce content for a full course merely because the resources to illustrate it are at hand. Yet is not the use of a text-book series, merely because of its availability, such an action? However expedient it may be, it is shirking our responsibilities to teach a course provided by a text-book series if it is contrary to our previously determined curriculum. If, by chance, a series provides a content and structure very similar to what we have already decided is worthwhile, then we are very lucky.

4 *A body of facts or values determined by . . . ?* If asked, most non-geographers would say that the job of the geography teacher was to teach a body of facts about the world. Clearly it is ludicrous to suggest that we should base what we teach on the views of those ignorant of our subject. No other discipline would contemplate the suggestion for a moment. The sad thing is that so many geographers too hold the view that our task is to teach facts about the world.

There are many reasons why this is a false and destructive aim. The obvious one is that facts are perpetually changing and expanding tremendously in quantity and complexity. What is the point in spending a great deal of time persuading young people to remember things which will be untrue within days, indeed hours? And where are the facts of geography to end? What do we exclude? With so many other methods of storing data available, why bother with the very inefficient one of the average person's memory? Rather, let us teach the pupil where relevant facts, whatever they are, may be obtained when needed.

There is then the difficult problem of what really constitutes a fact. If a pupil can quote that the capital of Norway is Oslo, or that the vegetation of much of northern Nigeria is savanna, does it mean anything if he does not understand what a capital city really is, or if he thinks savanna is dense forest? I have known pupils credited with knowing such facts in a test, yet their real ignorance has emerged in later discussion. We blithely convince ourselves that we are teaching facts when often we are merely getting pupils to learn word or diagram responses. There is clearly a need for much greater thought to be given to these vital issues than has been given in the past.

Even if there were agreement as to what constitutes facts, who would determine which facts should be selected from the truly enormous number available? Fact learning for its own sake seems a particularly pointless activity. Of course, facts have to be presented, understood, absorbed, checked and so on, but as a by-product of other activity. A content consisting of a body of facts is one based on a shallow understanding of the nature of geography and the nature of learning.

The problems of the desirability or otherwise of teaching attitudes or values – about world poverty, squalid urban environments, government control of locations, for example – are not easy to resolve. In spite of the difficulties of deciding which attitudes to teach, many teachers will see value in giving social purpose to some of their lessons. But again, it would be wrong to plan a course on the basis of a content of attitudes. It would certainly not be a course in geography.

5 *Suitability as a framework for using certain skills and techniques* In many ways this is the most insidious of the wrong reasons for choosing content. We may be so delighted with discovering a new method of collecting or analysing information that our course becomes merely a series of exercises in methodology. We might spend a complete course mapping land use, measuring traffic or pedestrian flow, drawing annotated sketches from slides or using Spearman's rank correlation coefficient. Yet this is false. Methods are designed to produce understanding about certain content or subject matter. They are subservient to content in every sense, and a content should never consist of a collection of techniques.

The most logical and useful basis for selecting content is:

6 *The fundamental body of ideas or concepts contained within geography as a discipline* The first chapter in Part 2 of this book indicated some of the developments in geography at university level. It is clear that the strength of the new geography is its greater concern with ideas and with the formulation and testing of geographical concepts. That such special concepts exist is the only justification for the subject – or at least for its being taken seriously by other people. Debate will long rage over whether such ideas are suitable for the immature minds of our pupils. The contention here is that it is not only possible for younger pupils to be introduced to them but also highly desirable.

If we are to have a subject-based curriculum, then we must do what this implies – teach geography. And that means teaching geographical ideas. It is held by many philosophers that the basic ideas of any subject can be appreciated by the very young if properly presented. Our problem is to decide what geographical ideas are worth teaching, and can also be understood by our pupils. It is nonsense to suggest that we must not allow people to think until they reach a certain point in their school life – no concepts before A-level. On the contrary we should try to instil the ideas at the earliest moment, and develop them as the pupil matures. Facts will be more relevant and more readily understood (and possibly even remembered) when introduced to illustrate or test an idea. Attitudes and values may also be discussed, when relevant to the theme.

There are further educational advantages in such an approach. The work will be more purposeful than that involved in learning the same type of fact – relief, climate, soils, etc. – by rote, time after time. Pupils who are made to think about geographical ideas and related themes are being more effectively prepared for an adult role in a rapidly changing society than they ever could be by learning a static body of facts. This surely will be high on the list of objectives in any school.

Our task is to list a number of geographical ideas. This involves selection and rejection, on the basis of what is in line with our stated objectives. These then have to be broken down into ideas to be introduced in each lesson. The fundamental principle is that the content or each lesson, and hence the total course, should be the geographical idea of concept we wish to teach. This should be the core of every single lesson, and we should always be quite clear what idea we are dealing with. A whole range of illustrative facts will be needed and methods used will be used to enable the pupils to understand the idea. But, as stated above, these are extras, a bonus to the understanding of an idea.

There is yet one more possible advantage in using this approach. If the core of any lesson is one idea it should be possible to devise methods of teaching so that all abilities can grasp it. Whatever content is chosen, this common core for all abilities is vitally necessary if non-streaming and the comprehensive need for mobility are to be anything other than shams. There is no need for the same method to be used with every ability range, nor indeed for the same area or example to be used as illustration. The aim of the lesson will be achieved if the idea is grasped. It is far more likely that this will happen than that a technique or large body of facts will be understood or learned by everyone.

Such is the belief. The content of our geography courses should be not facts, nor techniques, but geographical ideas. The practical problem is to decide on the ideas, in view of our constrained teaching circumstances, and on the order in which they should be handled.

Beddis's general position is accepted by John Everson who suggests devising new syllabuses by a 'matrix' scheme, in which fundamental concepts and the degrees of difficulty in teaching them are identified. The 'matrix' itself is not set out as a curriculum framework, but as a mental guide to the teacher who can design appropriate activities accordingly.

The organization of content – a suggested basis†

If by this stage a new geography exists and is worth while how do we introduce it into the schools in a comparatively painless way? If the regional approach adopted in most schools is not the organizational framework best suited to geography in its new guise, how do we alter the status quo? New geography involves the study of new material – settlements patterns, social and urban topics, for example; it also involves a scientific approach to data, the development of theory, and the use of generalizations, models and laws which enable us both to understand the complex world with its ever-increasing store of information and also to predict new ideas. It also involves the desire to include a random element in all human theory and the increasing interest in how people perceive their environment. Will this material and approach fit into the present framework of regional geography? As well as these pressures on what is taught there is the pressure of educational thinkers such as Bruner and Piaget and their views on how children learn. Here it is impossible to go into any detail, but a short summary of Bruner's views on curricula organization as applied to geography might include the following points:

1 The basic concepts of the subject, i.e. the structure of geography, are what a child really needs to know and facts are only important when they fit into this framework.
2 The basic concepts of the subject can be introduced at an early age and then refined and touched on again and again until the concept is fully understood. In this way the curricula can be regarded as a spiral continually turning in on itself and revisiting certain basic ideas.
3 Problem solving is the best way to show children how geographers think and to allow children to think as geographers think.
4 The work done should interest and motivate the child.
5 Discovery methods are one of the best ways of getting the child to understand the basic concepts of geography.

In addition to these factors, which put pressure on which curricular changes occur, there are also the organizational problems posed by the fact that many children today are taught in mixed ability groups. This has of course helped to develop the present trend towards individual and personalized work in geography. A further point to remember is that only about twenty per cent of our secondary school population ever take an examination in geography such as CSE or O-level, which means that very many children will have to get all the geography they will ever know by the time they choose their options at the end of the third or fourth year.

†John Everson

Once a decision has been made to revise the curriculum there are two main ways to progress. The syllabus can be looked at as a whole and an entirely new syllabus can be put into operation as with some of the many Nuffield schemes now in use in the schools. Or the designer can work the other way, and try by collecting small fragments of a course to build a whole curriculum stealthily. The second method is the one I shall suggest here. In passing let it be said that in future the need for continual revision of syllabuses, exams and curricula must be recognized. Change must be built into the system to avoid the necessity for traumatic changes after twenty or thirty years of slow ossification.

One strategy which we may find useful in creating the new syllabus is the adaptation of an idea of B. Banks (organizer of the West Kent Mathematical Project and a Nuffield research fellow). His approach was meant primarily for the organization of mathematics but an extension and development of his idea is valid I think in geography. This strategy envisages the division of what we want to teach the child into a series of topic areas. The areas suggested here are:

1 agriculture
2 transportation
3 landform processes
4 inside the city
5 settlement
6 political influences, local and national
7 meteorology and climate
8 vegetation and soils
9 population and under-development
10 location of industry and manufacturing

This division, it will be recognized, is a fairly traditional way of dividing up a fairly traditional view of the subject area of geography. These are considered to be the fields of study that should be covered in the secondary school. A primary school area of study might be described as a study of size, shape, direction and distance, and a matrix that involves developmental concepts in this area could be produced.

Once one has decided on the subject area to be studied it will be necessary to define the objectives of this particular area of geography. These objectives may be defined under three headings. Firstly, enquiry skills (these can be taken to be the structure of the subject): secondly, attitudes and values (the development of the student's views on conservation, planning, pollution, etc.); and lastly, knowledge (the facts that are necessary to test the theories). These objectives, however worthy, will be too vague to be of any use in day-to-day teaching and will have to be described in more detail and in behavioural terms if possible. It will probably be difficult to express attitudes and values in a behavioural way.

The next stage is to decide the basic concepts that are essential to an understanding of each area of the field of geography. For example, if one chooses settlements as the field of study one might choose the following concepts as the basic ones:

1 The settlement patterns of today depend in part on the patterns of earlier peoples and technology.
2 Favourable sites for settlement are governed by identifiable characteristics – health, safety and comfort, accessibility and to transport to resources are all favourable ones.
3 Parish shape and size is related to physical and economic factors and also to the nature of the settlement.
4 Intensity of land use around a settlement can vary according to the distance of the area from the settlement.
5 There is a regularity in the occurrence of different sized settlements in the area and a pattern in the location of the various sized settlements. There is an hierarchy of settlements according to population size.
6 All functions in a settlement have a threshold size which can be used to define a functional hierarchy which is related to the population hierarchy and the spacing of settlements.
7 Every settlement has a market area; its size is related to the settlement's size. Market areas nest and can be portrayed in an ideal hexagonal way.
8 Settlements grow and decline.
9 The interaction between settlements depends in part on the size of each centre.

Similarly the field inside the city might have the following concepts selected as the basic ones necessary for an understanding of this area.

1 Urban land users with different interests want to be near different things.
2 Time distance is a useful way to measure ease of access to a city.
3 Commercial land values tend to be high at accessible spots.
4 Different kinds of retail outlets display different locational characteristics.
5 Residential densities decrease as distance from the central business district increase.
6 Median family income, residential density and distance from central business district are related.
7 Cities prosper when money comes in by selling goods and services to people in other areas.
8 Cities grow through an increase in the number of employment possibilities.
9 Accessibility and growth are related. The more accessible the city is the better its chances for growth. Some typical land use patterns can evolve in cities.
10 City growth creates urban problems. Planning can relieve these problems.

The next step in the strategy is to build up a simple matrix with the concepts listed across the top, running from left to right in a possible developmental sequence. The vertical access shows the increasing difficulty to be found in one column i.e. concept. The difficulty level will express the complexity of the exercise or piece of work that is placed in this particular cell. This idea of difficulty will take into account such factors as the complexity of the statistics used, the difficulty of the map work required, the maturity of the child and the degree of abstraction required in the approach to the particular exercise. And the extent of the vertical axis of the matrix will depend on the aims of each matrix designer. One can imagine one matrix of, say, transportation created to cover the work of the entire school, or equally one can imagine separate matrices being constructed for lower middle and upper schools. A skeleton of a matrix is seen in fig. 42. The only problem now is the creation of pieces of

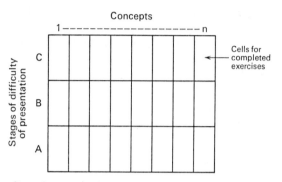

Fig 42. The outline of a matrix that could be used as a basis for planning a curriculum

work that demonstrate each concept at each difficulty level. However, many teachers already have a great number of exercises which could be directly 'hooked up' into one or other of the matrices. These would provide a beginning, while the matrix at once would point the way to further necessary work.

The exercises that will fill the cells of the matrices can be constructed on programmed learning lines if this type of self-testing material, closely defined, with clearly stated objectives, is appropriate to the work in hand.

A few examples of the exercises that we put into the cells can be given. The exercises will of course be varied; one cell may have a game in it, another a case study or a sample study, another a chapter from any book with questions (even multiple-choice questions) about the chapter. Others could be about the local area, a continent or the whole world. Other cells could contain a project, a piece of field work or field research, map work or statistics. And another cell could contain a piece of work to be done individually while yet another could demand discussion periods involving the whole class. The work in the cells should vary in approach, in scale of study (from the micro to the macro study) and in the techniques used. Through the matrix, as the child moves towards the top of the rows, the techniques used will develop towards more complex map work statistics and skills, as well as involving a more abstract approach to the concept being studied.

There are of course advantages and disadvantages in this approach to developing a new curriculum. The advantages include the basic one that the creation of a course of this type will be firmly based on theory and concept. Secondly, regional work or study of place will enter as the testing ground of the theory, while techniques such as mathematics, geometry and statistics and map work will be the means of testing and promoting further theory. At present there seems to be no other way of organizing geography so closely around its theoretical basis. The third advantage is that with a course of this kind, with much prepared work, the teacher will have more freedom to consider his children as individuals, as some of the work will be personal and individual. If a full programmed learning approach is used some of the work will be self-testing and this will further free the teacher and allow him to develop more personal relationships with the children. Fourthly, in a mixed ability class each child can progress on his own path through each matrix and also at his own speed. This will be of great help in many school situations, especially if some of the cells contain joint and class activities to relieve the strain of continued individual work. Fifthly, a course of this kind will help to overcome the problem of so many children giving up geography at the end of the third year (in some schools even earlier). This terminal point to their course is rarely satisfactory. They miss much map work and field work and all the ideas that are commonly introduced in the fourth and fifth years. Using this strategy the children will be able to sample the concepts we think are important, to whatever depth they are capable of, before they leave the subject for ever. Lastly, there are many courses proposed at present which involve geography in some form of organization with other subjects. Many schools now run courses called social studies or discovery or inter-departmental enquiry, which link up geography and history and perhaps English, religious education and mathematics. At the moment this new 'subject' is often of doubtful validity, as it has little organizational structure of its own. If geography were reorganized along conceptual lines, geographers could obviously enter more freely into these new subject areas, knowing, as they will do, what basic concepts are essential to a full geographical understanding of a particular area of knowledge.

Disadvantages certainly exist too. Does one study the matrices in any one particular order? How does one link up one matrix with another? If the children do individual work will the strain of accurate record-keeping be too great for busy secondary-school teachers? Will the child see the structure we are trying to create for him, or will he only see individual exercises that seem almost entirely unrelated to each other?

One idea now is that groups of teachers, based on perhaps local Geographical Association branches or the teachers' centre, will get together to decide on their objectives and concepts. They will then build up matrices for themselves. Some time it may be possible through the Models and Quantitative Techniques Committee of the Geographical Association to collect these attempts and to circulate a group's work generally. Presumably each group's concepts will vary: but even if the groups agree on the basic concepts, the actual exercises will vary, although they will lead to the same ends. At this stage it might be possible to say that we have created a new and very flexible geography course, built up of the various parts contributed by the groups. It might then be possible to replace the present regional approach by this newer one or to run the two systems in tandem for some years until the value of the matrix approach can be fully assessed.

Everson's suggestion is that concepts are best organized on a basis of systematic topics. Rex Beddis, on the other hand, argues for the retention of 'area-based studies'. He argues that concepts are best revised and reintroduced in different contexts and that a sense of place is one to which pupils respond readily. It is apparent, however, that this kind of concept-based area study is somewhat different from the overall coverage objectives of much traditional regional geography.

The case for an areal structure†

Reaction against traditional regional geography is so strong that there is a danger that an areal structure might be rejected without its case being clearly stated. Yet the regional and areal structures are quite distinct, and it is a mistake to link them in any way.

It has been claimed earlier that the basic content of any lesson should be a geographical idea or concept. Even when the ideas and concepts are agreed upon a decision has to be made about the order in which they are presented. It is sensible to arrange for simple ideas to be introduced before complex ones, for example. It is also sensible for ideas to be reintroduced, revised and developed at intervals throughout the course.

One suggestion is that the ideas from a particular branch of the subject, say, urban geography, should be introduced in a slab of perhaps one term. Examples to illustrate the ideas will be taken from all over the world, showing the universality of many processes and forms. This will be followed by another set of ideas from another branch, say agricultural geography. Another possibility is to take a set of ideas around a concept, such as networks, and to deal with these for a period of time. It certainly allows time to get absorbed with the ideas, for one is not flitting from one set of ideas to another every lesson. On the other hand these structures pose several major problems. For example, how can one justify taking one particular set of ideas in term one and withholding another set for several years? Is there a hierarchy of difficulty between sets of ideas? Linked to this is the other problem of how to ensure revision and development at a subsequent stage without fragmenting the later work. It is because of such problems – and also because of several positive advantages – that an areal structure is proposed as an alternative.

†Rex Beddis

186

The principle is quite simply that the lessons for any one term would
(a) consist of ideas from a very wide range of branches of the subject
(b) be illustrated with examples taken primarily (but not exclusively) from one area, possibly one continent.

Only at the later stage of a course would themes be treated systematically, and then as consolidation, and in conjunction with more advanced areal studies.

The area used for illustrative material in, say, year four, might be western Europe. The following scheme suggests how, within a term, six lessons might be developed with illustrations from France.

Lesson theme The influence of the physical environment on farm patterns and systems.

Area examples Finisterre, Sarthe, and Haut Rhin in North France.

Lesson theme The influence of type of tenure on farm systems. Fragmentation and consolidation.

Area examples Beauce and the Central Plateau.

Lesson theme The climatic region. Problems of delimitation.

Area example The Mediterranean region of France.

Lesson theme Where does a city end? The physical boundaries of towns.

Area example Toulouse.

Lesson theme Where does a city end? Spheres of influence.

Area examples The major town and cities of France.

Lesson theme The processes and problems of urban growth. Internal movements.

Area example The new urban motorway system of Paris.

Note:
1 There may be a number of ancillary themes, depending on the nature of the class which is being taught.
2 There should be frequent cross-reference to other similar (or contradictory) examples, including those in the local area. The unique quality should not be stressed.
3 The French situation may well have been used earlier, or may be planned for later use, in connection with other themes. For example, ideas of industrial location introduced in a study of the Ruhr would probably also include data on the industrial areas of northern France.
4 This may not be the first time that these ideas have been introduced. There is a need for frequent reference to past examples and discussions on the themes.
5 The whole range of teaching methods and aids may be used. Variety from lesson to lesson should be the keynote, e.g. a theme might be introduced through a game and tested in the local area.
6 Discussion of values and attitudes can be introduced where relevant, e.g. the arguments for and against urban motorways.

It may be argued that such a structure fragments the sets of ideas too much, and that as soon as one becomes acquainted with the nature of farming systems one is off on a theme about formal regions. Soon after that, the ideas concern towns. In view of the fragmented nature of most lessons, separated by days, this may not be as disastrous as it sounds. The ability to deal with this wide range of ideas in every term, illustrated from all continents, enables the principle of continuous revision and development to be practised easily.

Another point in its favour is that many ideas require an understanding of the importance of decision making, and nowadays many of the most significant decisions are taken by the governments of nations. There are good reasons for studying the states as political units, and seeing the functionally linked parts of the economy of a country.

Although it is impossible to prove, a case could be made that pupils can see better the way phenomena are related in space if they consider the same space for some length of time, particularly if it illustrates different ideas. The continual switching of interest from farm, to town, to area, to state, to continent and back again should make the pupil more aware of the significance of scale.

It may be that all these claims, and more, could be made for alternative structures. There may also be severe and positive criticism of areal structure. The point is that the proposal deserves a hearing, and it may prove the basis of a suitable structure for the new geography in schools.

[Editor's note: This issue is also sensitively pursued in general terms by W. R. Mead in Chapter 23 of *Trends in Geography*, ed R. U. Cooke and J. H. Johnson, Pergamon.]

Acknowledgements

We are grateful to the following for permission to reproduce copyright material:

The Geographical Association for the following from various *Geography* magazines: an extract from 'Memorandum re Geography Teaching', January 1962; an extract from an article by J. W. Morris in Vol. 51(4) 1966; an extract from the review section by P. R. C., Nov. 1968, Vol. 54 (4), and an extract from the article by N. Ginsburg, Nov. 1969, in Vol. 54 (4); Joint Matriculation Board for material from the *Board's Occasional Publication 29*; Oxford and Cambridge Schools Examination Board for quotations from the explanatory notes from their *A-level Geography syllabus*, 1969; Professor N. V. Scarfe for extracts from two articles in *Journal of Geography*, in Vol. LXIV No. 4, Apr. 1965 and Vol. 67, Jan. 1968 respectively and Yorkshire Regional Examinations Board for an extract from the *Research Report No. 5, 1968*.

Index

Index

The many places around which exercises have been developed are omitted from the index, since they are considered incidental to the subject-matter of this book.